# COOKING VEGETARIAN

# CONTENTS

EDITORIAL
Food Editor Sheryle Eastwood
US Copy Editor Diane Hodges
Assistant Food Editor Rachel Blackmore
Home Economist Anneka Mitchell
Recipe Development Jane Ash, Penny Cox,
Sue Geraghty, Meg Thorley
Food Consultant Frances Naldrett
Nutrition Consultant Helen O'Connor
Text Denise Greig, Alison Magney
Editorial Coordinators Margaret Kelly, Claire Pallant
Subeditor Ella Martin

PHOTOGRAPHY
Yanto Noriento

STYLING
Wendy Berecry
Marie Hélène Clauzon

ILLUSTRATIONS
Jill MacLeod
PRODUCTION
Tracy Burt, Margie Mulray, Chris Hatcher

DESIGN AND PRODUCTION MANAGER
Nadia Sbisa

PUBLISHER
Philippa Sandall

Published by J.B. Fairfax Press Inc.,
a wholly owned subsidiary of J.B. Fairfax
International

COOKING VEGETARIAN – Light, Easy, and
Imaginative Meatless Meals
Includes Index
ISBN 1 56197 022 0
Formatted by J.B. Fairfax Press Pty Ltd
Printed by Toppan Printing Co., Singapore

## CHECK-AND-GO

When planning a meal, use the easy Check-and-Go boxes which appear beside each ingredient. Simply check on your pantry shelf and if the ingredients are not there, tick the boxes as a reminder to add those items to your shopping list.

### METRIC MEASURES

| | |
|---|---|
| 1.25 mL | $^1/_4$ teaspoon |
| 2.5 mL | $^1/_2$ teaspoon |
| 5 mL | 1 teaspoon |
| 20 mL | 1 tablespoon |
| 60 mL | $^1/_4$ cup |
| 80 mL | $^1/_3$ cup |
| 125 mL | $^1/_2$ cup |
| 250 mL | 1 cup |

# FOOD
## *for thought*

Fresh, light, delicious – these are not words that many people associate with vegetarianism. That is, until now. Vegetarianism has, for far too long, been associated in people's minds with "gluggy" bowls of brown rice, plates of boiled lentils, indigestible slabs of "good-for-you" pies which, rather than being feather light and delectable, sit on your stomach for hours. Banish those ideas forever.

The influence of Asian cooking styles, such as stir-frying and steaming, have been eagerly embraced by imaginative vegetarian cooks, with the result that vibrantly colored vegetables, stir-fried in a flash, sprinkled with cilantro (fresh coriander) leaves and accompanied by a little steamed Basmati rice are winning over traditional meat eaters.

Today, people are increasingly turning to delicious, inexpensive and healthy vegetarian fare as an alternative to the traditional meaty main dishes. Whether you want occasional meatless meals or a completely vegetarian diet, you will find many imaginative suggestions in this beautifully photographed book.

More than ever before, people want to experience their natural energy, and to simply feel "good". Light, meatless eating is one widely acknowledged way to achieve this goal.

Vegetarian diets are usually lower in fat and higher in fiber than diets which include meat. Seventh Day Adventists, who eat a varied vegetarian diet, have a good health record. They are less likely to be overweight and they have fewer people with heart disease, high blood pressure and cancer compared with the rest of the population. However, it must also be remembered that they lead a generally healthy lifestyle and neither smoke nor drink alcohol.

Well-balanced vegetarian diets are now known to be nutritionally adequate, especially those that include milk and eggs. Very severe diets can be a problem, although with careful planning these too can be nutritionally sound. Strict macrobiotic or fruitarian diets (fruit only) cannot provide all the nutrients you need for good health.

When planning a vegetarian diet, you must be careful to include the nutrients you need for good health. This is especially important for children and for pregnant women and breastfeeding mothers, who have greater nutritional needs. Because of the bulky nature of the vegetarian diet, children sometimes cannot eat enough energy and protein. However, this is less likely to be a problem in diets which include milk and eggs.

Vegetarianism suffered from a reputation of seriousness, in the bad old days, but now, innovation and fun are the key words. You'll be astounded at the variety of cooking styles and ingredients that this book introduces, and the bold, different ways in which these ingredients have been put together.

If you are "new" to vegetarianism, look at our chapters on Vegetarian Foods Explained, Vegetarian Essentials and Easy Menu Planning for advice and inspiration.

If you are not new to vegetarianism, a quick look through our recipes might well take you back to the culinary drawing board!

Welcome to the new vegetarianism – you have nothing to lose but your old prejudices.

In recent years there has been a renewed interest in vegetarianism. Although cultural and religious groups have practiced vegetarianism for centuries, an increasing number of people are now adopting a vegetarian diet for a variety of reasons: philosophical, economical, religious, humanitarian, health or ecological.

Given that "meat on the plate" has traditionally been a sign of aristocracy or wealth, it is interesting to find that the vegetarian diet is now an acceptable, even fashionable, alternative. This attitude is far from the traditional view of vegetarians who were often labeled as eccentrics or lunatics!

If you want to eat a vegetarian diet, variety and balance are the keys to success, as for all diets. If you are just adopting a vegetarian diet, it is a good idea to modify your eating habits gradually as you become more familiar with the diet. Since the vegetarian diet is high in complex carbohydrate and fiber, low in fat and refined sugars, it embraces many of the dietary guidelines for good health. Given this and the increased social acceptance of vegetarianism, perhaps more people will experiment with vegetarian-style meals, or at least increased amounts of vegetables and fruits in their diet.

## DO YOU KNOW?

Which of the following were vegetarian?

☐ Pythagoras
☐ William Shakespeare
☐ Aristotle
☐ Charles Dickens
☐ John Milton
☐ George Bernard Shaw

Answer: Pythagoras, Aristotle, John Milton, George Bernard Shaw

*A little taste of something delicious is good for the soul, not to mention children's morning break at school, mid-afternoon in a frantic office, or whenever time is short and food is needed.*

# TASTY TOPPERS
## *and fancy fillers*

### ❖
### FRUITY BANANA AND CAMEMBERT MUFFINS

*This combination of fruit and cheese is sure to be a popular snack.*

Serves 4

- [ ] 1 large banana, peeled and sliced
- [ ] $1/2$ green apple, cored and chopped
- [ ] $1/2$ stalk celery, sliced
- [ ] 3 tablespoons chopped pecans
- [ ] 2 teaspoons dry grated coconut
- [ ] 2 tablespoons mayonnaise
- [ ] 4 fruit muffins, halved and buttered
- [ ] 4 oz (125 g) Camembert cheese, sliced

Combine banana, apple, celery, pecans, coconut and mayonnaise. Spoon onto muffin halves and top with Camembert slices. Broil under medium heat until cheese melts. Serve immediately.

### ❖
### CHILI BEAN TACOS

*Tacos are always a welcome light meal or snack, and these delicious bean-filled ones take next to no time to prepare.*

Serves 4

- [ ] 14 oz (440 g) canned red kidney beans, drained and rinsed
- [ ] 1 teaspoon ground cumin
- [ ] 1 tomato, peeled and chopped
- [ ] 1 teaspoon chili sauce
- [ ] 8 taco shells
- [ ] 4 lettuce leaves, shredded
- [ ] shredded Cheddar cheese

1   Place kidney beans, cumin, tomato and chili sauce in a saucepan and cook over medium heat for 3-4 minutes or until heated through.
2   Arrange taco shells on a cookie sheet and heat at 350°F (180°C) for 5 minutes or until heated through. Fill taco shells with bean mixture.
3   Top with shredded lettuce and cheese. Serve immediately.

### ❖
### FRENCH ONION ROLLS

Serves 4

- [ ] 4 wholewheat rolls
- [ ] 1 tablespoon (15 g) margarine
- [ ] 1 large onion, sliced
- [ ] 2 eggs, lightly beaten
- [ ] $1/2$ cup (125 g) dairy sour cream
- [ ] 3 tablespoons evaporated skim milk
- [ ] $1/2$ teaspoon ground nutmeg
- [ ] 1 teaspoon horseradish cream
- [ ] freshly ground black pepper
- [ ] 1 cup (125 g) shredded Cheddar cheese

1   Scoop out center of rolls, leaving about $1/2$-inch (1 cm) thick shell. Place rolls on a cookie sheet and set aside.
2   Melt margarine in a skillet and cook onion for 4-5 minutes or until golden. Divide onion between rolls.
3   Place eggs, sour cream, skim milk, nutmeg and horseradish cream in a bowl. Mix to combine and season to taste with pepper. Spoon egg mixture into rolls, top with cheese and bake at 400°F (200°C) for 20-25 minutes or until firm.

*Fruity Banana and Camembert Muffins, Chili Bean Tacos, French Onion Rolls*

Plates Made in Japan

# DEVILED SOUFFLE MUSHROOM CAPS

Serves 4

- ☐ 8 large flat open mushrooms, stems removed and chopped
- ☐ 2 tablespoons (30 g) margarine, melted

DEVILED FILLING
- ☐ 1 tablespoon (15 g) margarine
- ☐ 4 tablespoons slivered almonds
- ☐ 1 green pepper, seeded and finely chopped
- ☐ 1½ teaspoons curry powder
- ☐ 1½ teaspoons dry mustard
- ☐ 2 teaspoons brown sugar
- ☐ 2 tablespoons catsup
- ☐ 1 teaspoon Worcestershire sauce

SOUFFLE TOPPING
- ☐ 2 egg whites
- ☐ 1 tablespoon mayonnaise
- ☐ 4 tablespoons shredded Cheddar cheese

1   Wipe mushroom caps and brush with margarine and place, cap-side down, on a cookie sheet.
2   To make filling: Melt margarine in a skillet and cook almonds until golden. Add pepper and mushroom stems and stir-fry for 2 minutes. Stir in curry powder, mustard and brown sugar, cook for 1 minute. Add catsup and Worcestershire sauce. Cook until just heated through, then remove pan from heat. Divide filling between mushroom caps.
3   To make soufflé topping: Beat egg whites until stiff peaks form. Fold into mayonnaise and spoon mixture over mushrooms. Top with cheese and bake at 425°F (220°C) for 8-10 minutes.

❖

# CURRIED LETTUCE ROLLS

Serves 4

- ☐ 2 tablespoons (30 g) margarine
- ☐ 1 tablespoon curry powder
- ☐ 1 onion, chopped
- ☐ 2 stalks celery, chopped
- ☐ 2 large ripe tomatoes, peeled and chopped
- ☐ 1 red pepper, seeded and chopped
- ☐ 14 oz (440 g) canned red kidney beans, drained and rinsed
- ☐ freshly ground black pepper
- ☐ 8 large iceberg lettuce leaves, blanched

DRESSING
- ☐ 1 tablespoon olive oil
- ☐ 3 tablespoons red wine vinegar
- ☐ 1 tablespoon tomato paste
- ☐ 1 tablespoon chopped cilantro (fresh coriander) leaves
- ☐ ¼ teaspoon ground cumin
- ☐ freshly ground black pepper

1   Melt margarine in a saucepan and cook curry powder, onion and celery for 3 minutes. Stir in tomatoes, pepper and kidney beans. Cover and simmer for 15 minutes or until thick. Season to taste with pepper. Spoon bean mixture onto lettuce leaves and roll up firmly to secure.
2   To make dressing: place oil, vinegar, tomato paste, cilantro and cumin in a screwtop jar and shake well to combine. Season to taste with pepper. To serve: Drizzle dressing over rolls.

*Devilled Soufflé Mushroom Caps, Curried Lettuce Rolls*

Plates Les Olivades

*Tomato and Mozzarella Pizza Subs, Pita Pizza Roll-Ups, Nachos*

❖

## TOMATO AND MOZZARELLA PIZZA SUBS

*Ideal for after-school fare.*

Serves 2

- ☐ **2 long wholewheat rolls, split and toasted**
- ☐ **2 tablespoons tomato paste**
- ☐ **1 small onion, finely sliced**
- ☐ **1 tablespoon finely chopped fresh basil**
- ☐ **4 black olives, pitted and sliced**
- ☐ **1 tablespoon pine nuts**
- ☐ **¹/4 cup ( 30 g) shredded mozzarella cheese**
- ☐ **freshly ground black pepper**

1   Spread each half roll with tomato paste. Top with onion, then sprinkle with basil, olives, pine nuts and cheese. Season to taste with pepper.

2   Broil under medium heat for 4-5 minutes, or until cheese melts.

❖

## NACHOS

Serves 4

- ☐ **5 oz (155 g) corn chips**
- ☐ **2 tomatoes, peeled and finely chopped**
- ☐ **1 cup (125 g) shredded mozzarella cheese**
- ☐ **1 cup (125 g) shredded Cheddar cheese**

AVOCADO TOPPING
- ☐ **2 small avocados, pitted, peeled, and chopped**
- ☐ **2 teaspoons lemon juice**
- ☐ **1 small onion, grated**
- ☐ **2 cloves garlic, crushed**
- ☐ **1 teaspoon chili sauce**

1   Layer corn chips, tomatoes and cheeses in an ovenproof dish, finishing with a layer of cheese. Bake at 400°F (200°C) for 10-15 minutes, or until cheese melts.

2   To make topping: Place avocados, lemon juice, onion, garlic and chili sauce in a food processor or blender and process until smooth. Spoon onto corn chips and serve immediately.

❖

## PITA PIZZA ROLL-UPS

Serves 6

- ☐ **3 tablespoons tomato paste**
- ☐ **2 tablespoons finely chopped fresh basil**
- ☐ **3 tablespoons chopped pitted black olives**
- ☐ **6 large pita bread rounds**
- ☐ **6¹/2 oz (200 g) mushrooms, finely chopped**
- ☐ **1 small red pepper, finely sliced**
- ☐ **1 onion, chopped**
- ☐ **1³/4 cups (200 g) ricotta cheese**
- ☐ **1³/4 cups (200 g) shredded mozzarella cheese**

1   Combine tomato paste, basil and olives. Divide mixture into six portions and spread over pita bread. Top with mushrooms, pepper, onion and ricotta cheese. Press down lightly, then roll up tightly and secure with a toothpick.

2   Place rolls on a cookie sheet and sprinkle with mozzarella cheese. Bake at 425°F (220°C) for 15-20 minutes, or until heated through and cheese melts.

❖

## SPINACH SLAW

Serves 4

- ☐ 8 oz (250 g) spinach leaves, finely shredded
- ☐ 1 carrot, peeled and shredded
- ☐ 1/2 cup (100 g) golden raisins
- ☐ 2/3 cup (100 g) roasted peanuts, chopped
- ☐ 1/2 cup (125 g) mayonnaise
- ☐ freshly ground black pepper

Combine spinach, carrot, golden raisins, peanuts and mayonnaise. Season to taste with freshly ground black pepper.

❖

## CARAWAY SLAW TOPPING

Serves 4

- ☐ 1/4 head small cabbage, shredded
- ☐ 2 teaspoons caraway seeds
- ☐ 2 teaspoons coarse grain mustard

- ☐ 1 tablespoon mayonnaise
- ☐ 8 slices Swiss cheese
- ☐ 4 dill pickles, sliced lengthwise

Combine cabbage, caraway seeds, mustard and mayonnaise. Divide between four slices of bread, then top each slice with 2 slices of cheese and 2 slices of dill pickles.

❖

## COOL CUCUMBER TOPPING

Serves 4

- ☐ 1 English cucumber, peeled and diced
- ☐ 1/2 cup (125 g) plain low-fat yogurt
- ☐ 1 tablespoon finely chopped fresh dill

Combine cucumber, yogurt and dill.

❖

## GORGONZOLA AND WALNUTS

Serves 4

- ☐ 1³/4 cups (200 g) Gorgonzola cheese, mashed
- ☐ 4 oz (125 g) walnuts, chopped
- ☐ 8 Romaine lettuce leaves
- ☐ 1 oz (30 g) alfalfa sprouts

Combine Gorgonzola cheese and walnuts. Line pita pockets, or top bread slices, with lettuce leaves, then top with Gorgonzola mixture and alfalfa sprouts.

❖

## CHEESE ASPARAGUS TOPPING

Serves 4

- ☐ 10 oz (315 g) canned asparagus tips, drained
- ☐ 1 teaspoon coarse grain mustard
- ☐ 1 tablespoon mayonnaise
- ☐ 1/2 cup (60 g) Gorgonzola cheese, crumbled

Place asparagus, mustard and mayonnaise in a small bowl and mash to combine. Spread over four slices of bread and sprinkle with cheese.

*Variation*

You might like to place this topping on toasted bread, then broil and serve hot.

## GARDEN FRESH VEGETABLE AND SALAD PLATTER

*This platter is ideal to serve as a light meal, snack or starter for a barbecue.*

Serves 4

- ☐ 4 slices Cheddar cheese
- ☐ 1 large tomato, cut into sixths
- ☐ 1 small cucumber, peeled and cut into thin strips
- ☐ 8 canned asparagus spears
- ☐ 8 radishes
- ☐ 2 hard-cooked eggs, sliced
- ☐ 5 oz (155 g) button mushrooms, sliced
- ☐ 1 large stalk celery, cut into thin strips

DILL DIPPING SAUCE
- ☐ 2 tablespoons mayonnaise
- ☐ 1/2 cup (125 g) plain low-fat yogurt
- ☐ 1 teaspoon grated lemon rind
- ☐ 2 tablespoons finely chopped fresh dill

1  Arrange cheese slices, tomato, cucumber, asparagus, radishes, eggs, mushrooms and celery attractively on a platter.

2  To make sauce: Combine mayonnaise, yogurt, lemon rind and dill in a bowl. Mix well to combine and serve with vegetable and salad platter.

## CANTALOUPE CAMEMBERT TOPPING

Serves 4

- ☐ French mustard
- ☐ arugula leaves
- ☐ 125 g (4 oz) Camembert cheese, sliced
- ☐ 1/2 small cantaloupe, peeled, seeded and diced

1  Spread each slice of bread with French mustard to taste.

2  Top with arugula leaves, Camembert cheese and cantaloupe.

## MEXICAN PUMPKIN SEED DIP

*You might like to serve this dip on a vegetable platter in place of (or as well as) the Dill Dipping Sauce.*

Serves 6

- ☐ 3 1/2 oz (100 g) Mexican pumpkin seeds, toasted
- ☐ 1 tablespoon lemon juice
- ☐ 2 tablespoons balsamic vinegar
- ☐ 1 clove garlic, crushed
- ☐ 1/2 teaspoon Dijon-style mustard

Place toasted pumpkin seeds, lemon juice, vinegar, garlic and mustard in a food processor or blender and process until smooth. Chill before serving.

## TOMATOES AND MOZZARELLA

Serves 4

- ☐ 4 tomatoes, chopped
- ☐ 1 cup (125 g) mozzarella cheese, cubed
- ☐ 2 tablespoons finely chopped fresh basil
- ☐ 3 1/2 oz (100 g) pitted black olives
- ☐ 2 tablespoons cider vinegar
- ☐ 1 tablespoon olive oil
- ☐ freshly ground black pepper

Combine tomatoes, cheese, basil and olives. Mix together vinegar and oil, pour over tomato mixture and toss to combine. Season to taste with black pepper and use as desired.

*From left: Toppers and fillings on a selection of bread: Spinach Slaw, Gorgonzola and Walnuts, Cantaloupe Camembert Topping, Cheese Asparagus Topping, Caraway Slaw Topping, Tomatoes and Mozzarella, Cool Cucumber Topping, Garden Fresh Vegetable and Salad Platter, Mexican Pumpkin Seed Dip*

*A tasty soup or starter can really tantalize your taste buds. This chapter shows you how to make mouthwatering starters and side dishes for all occasions.*

# SUPER STARTERS
## *and sensational sides*

❖

### SPINACH AND TOMATO CREPE BAKE

Serves 6

- ☐ **4 tablespoons wholewheat plain flour, sifted and grits returned**
- ☐ **4 tablespoons buckwheat flour, sifted**
- ☐ **1 egg, lightly beaten**
- ☐ **1 cup (250 mL) milk**
- ☐ **1 tablespoon vegetable oil**

FILLING

- ☐ **16 oz (500 g) spinach washed, stalks removed and leaves chopped**
- ☐ **1 tablespoon (15 g) margarine**
- ☐ **1 onion, finely chopped**
- ☐ **12 oz (375 g) ricotta cheese**
- ☐ **1 tablespoon grated Parmesan cheese**
- ☐ **¹/₂ teaspoon ground nutmeg**
- ☐ **2 oz (60 g) pine nuts, toasted**
- ☐ **freshly ground black pepper**
- ☐ **³/₄ cup (90 g) shredded Cheddar cheese**

TOMATO SAUCE

- ☐ **4 fl oz (125 mL) vegetable stock**
- ☐ **14 oz (440 g) canned tomatoes, undrained and mashed**
- ☐ **1 tablespoon tomato paste**
- ☐ **¹/₂ teaspoon sugar**
- ☐ **1 tablespoon finely chopped fresh basil**

1  Combine wholewheat and buckwheat flours in a bowl. Whisk together egg, milk and oil. Gradually add to flour mixture and mix to a smooth batter. Cover and set aside for 30 minutes. Pour 2-3 tablespoons of batter into a greased and heated, small heavy skillet or crêpe pan and cook until lightly browned on each side. Repeat with remaining batter.

2  To make filling: Boil, steam or microwave spinach until tender. Drain well and set aside. Melt margarine in a saucepan and cook onion for 5 minutes or until softened. Place spinach, onion, ricotta cheese, Parmesan cheese, nutmeg and pine nuts in a bowl. Mix to combine. Season to taste with pepper.

3  Spoon spinach mixture into center of crêpes and roll up. Place in a lightly greased baking dish and sprinkle with Cheddar cheese. Bake at 350°F (180°C) for 25 minutes, or until heated through.

4  To make sauce: Place stock, tomatoes, tomato paste, sugar and basil in a saucepan and cook for 5 minutes or until sauce thickens. Spoon over crêpes and serve.

❖

### MINTED PEA AND WATERCRESS SOUP

Serves 4

- ☐ **1 oz (30 g) margarine**
- ☐ **1 onion, finely chopped**
- ☐ **1 clove garlic, crushed**
- ☐ **1 bunch watercress, chopped**
- ☐ **8 oz (250 g) frozen green peas**
- ☐ **3 cups (750 mL) vegetable stock or broth**
- ☐ **freshly ground black pepper**
- ☐ **2 tablespoons finely chopped fresh mint**
- ☐ **4 tablespoons plain low-fat yogurt**

1  Melt margarine in a large saucepan and cook onion and garlic for 3-4 minutes. Stir in watercress, peas and stock or broth. Bring to the boil, reduce heat, cover and simmer for 15 minutes. Season to taste.

2  Transfer soup to a food processor or blender and process until smooth. Return to a clean saucepan, stir in mint and heat for 2-3 minutes. Serve hot, or chilled, in individual bowls with a swirl of yogurt.

❖

### THAI VEGETABLE PUFFS WITH DIPPING SAUCE

*Spice-laden, savory-filled parcels served with a traditional Thai dipping sauce.*

Makes 24

- ☐ **12 oz (375 g) prepared or ready-rolled puff pastry, thawed**
- ☐ **vegetable oil for deep frying**

FILLING

- ☐ **2 tablespoons (30 g) margarine**
- ☐ **1 teaspoon curry powder**
- ☐ **¹/₂ teaspoon ground cumin**
- ☐ **¹/₂ teaspoon garam masala**
- ☐ **1 small onion, finely chopped**
- ☐ **1 large carrot, peeled and shredded**
- ☐ **1 zucchini, shredded**
- ☐ **1 tablespoon crunchy peanut butter**
- ☐ **2 large potatoes, cooked and mashed**

DIPPING SAUCE

- ☐ **1 cup (250 mL) vinegar**
- ☐ **³/₄ cup (185 g) sugar**
- ☐ **1 small red chili, seeded and finely chopped**
- ☐ **1 small cucumber, peeled, seeded and finely chopped**

1  Roll out pastry to ¹/₈-inch (3 mm) thickness. Using a 3-inch (7.5 cm) round pastry cutter, cut 24 pastry rounds.

2  To make filling: Melt margarine in a saucepan, stir in curry powder, cumin and garam masala and cook for 1 minute. Add onion, carrot and zucchini and cook until vegetables are tender. Stir in peanut butter and combine with potatoes.

3  Lay a pastry round in the palm of your hand and place a teaspoon of filling in the center. Wet edge of the pastry with a little water, fold pastry over filling and pinch edges to seal. Repeat with remaining pastry rounds and filling.

4  To make sauce: Place vinegar and sugar in a small saucepan and cook over low heat, stirring frequently, without boiling, until sugar dissolves. Mix in chili and cucumber, bring to the boil, then reduce heat and simmer uncovered for 5 minutes or until sauce thickens slightly.

5  Heat oil in a large saucepan and cook puffs for 3-4 minutes or until crisp and golden. Drain on paper towels and serve with dipping sauce.

*Thai Vegetable Puffs with Dipping Sauce, Minted Pea and Watercress Soup, Savory Avocados with Pistachios (page 14), Spinach and Tomato Crêpe Bake*

## SAVORY AVOCADOS WITH PISTACHIOS

*Avocado lovers will enjoy these tangy filled avocados as a starter or light meal. Make the filling in advance, but leave the assembly until shortly before serving.*

Serves 6

- ☐ **3 avocados, halved, pitted and peeled**
- ☐ **1 tablespoon lemon juice**
- ☐ **2 tablespoons roughly chopped unsalted pistachio nuts**

FILLING
- ☐ **1 large zucchini, shredded**
- ☐ **2 tablespoons finely chopped fresh mint**
- ☐ **2 tablespoons roughly chopped unsalted pistachio nuts**
- ☐ **2 tablespoons dairy sour cream**
- ☐ **2 tablespoons lime juice**
- ☐ **freshly ground black pepper**

1  Brush cut surfaces of avocados with lemon juice, cover and set aside.
2  To make filling: Place zucchini, mint and pistachios in a bowl. Whisk together sour cream and lime juice and pour into zucchini mixture. Toss to combine. Season with pepper.
3  Spoon zucchini filling into avocados and sprinkle with pistachios.

## SPINACH TIMBALES WITH SPICY PEAR SAUCE

*These deep green timbales look sensational when served with the pale Spicy Pear Sauce, and as a final touch you might like to garnish the plate with a fanned pear slice! Great as a starter or light meal.*

Serves 4

- ☐ **16 oz (500 g) spinach leaves, roughly chopped**
- ☐ **3 eggs**
- ☐ **1/2 cup (125 mL) light cream**
- ☐ **pinch ground nutmeg**
- ☐ **freshly ground black pepper**

SPICY PEAR SAUCE
- ☐ **2 ripe pears, peeled, cored and coarsely chopped**
- ☐ **2 tablespoons light cream**
- ☐ **1/2 teaspoon chili sauce**
- ☐ **pinch ground nutmeg**

1  Boil, steam or microwave spinach until tender. Refresh under cold running water and drain thoroughly. Squeeze spinach to remove excess liquid. Place in food processor or blender and process until smooth. Add eggs, cream, nutmeg and pepper to taste and process again until all ingredients are combined.
2  Spoon spinach mixture into four greased individual timbale molds (1/2 cup/ 125 mL capacity), cover with aluminum foil and place in a baking dish. Pour in boiling water to come halfway up the sides of the molds. Bake at 350°F (180°C) for 40-45 minutes or until set. Remove from water and leave 5 minutes before turning out.
3  To make sauce: Place pears, cream, chili sauce and nutmeg in food processor or blender and process until smooth. Transfer to a small saucepan and heat gently for 3-4 minutes, or until the sauce is just warm. Serve with timbales.

---

### COOK'S TIP
If fresh pears are unavailable, canned pears in natural juice can be used as a substitute.

---

## CORN AND CHILI SOUFFLE

Serves 4

- ☐ **2 oz (60 g) margarine**
- ☐ **1 onion, finely chopped**
- ☐ **1 red chili pepper, seeded and finely chopped**
- ☐ **3 tablespoons all-purpose flour**
- ☐ **1/2 cup (125 mL) milk**
- ☐ **10 oz (315 g) canned creamed corn**
- ☐ **4 egg yolks, lightly beaten**
- ☐ **freshly ground black pepper**
- ☐ **5 egg whites**
- ☐ **3 tablespoons bread crumbs made from stale bread**

1  Melt margarine in a saucepan and cook onion and chili over medium heat for 10 minutes, or until onion is soft and golden. Stir in flour and cook for 1 minute. Remove from heat and gradually stir in milk and corn. Return to heat and cook, stirring constantly, until mixture boils and thickens. Remove from heat and beat in egg yolks. Season to taste with pepper.
2  Place egg whites in a medium bowl and beat until stiff peaks form. Fold gently into corn mixture.
3  Grease a 7-inch (18 cm) soufflé dish and sprinkle with bread crumbs. Grease a paper collar, sprinkle with bread crumbs and attach to soufflé dish.
4  Spoon soufflé mixture into prepared dish and bake at 400°F (200°C) for 30-35 minutes or until puffed and browned. Serve immediately.

*Corn and Chili Soufflé*

## SWEET POTATO SOUP WITH GINGER AND LIME

Serves 4

- ☐ **2 tablespoons (30 g) polyunsaturated margarine**
- ☐ **1 onion, finely chopped**
- ☐ **1 clove garlic, crushed**
- ☐ **1¹/₂ teaspoons grated fresh ginger**
- ☐ **1¹/₂ lb (750 g) sweet potato, peeled and cut into chunks**
- ☐ **4 cups (1 litre) vegetable stock or water**
- ☐ **2 tablespoons lime juice**
- ☐ **ground white pepper**

1   Melt margarine in a saucepan and cook onion, garlic and ginger for 2-3 minutes or until soft. Add sweet potato and stock. Bring to the boil, then reduce heat and simmer for 15-20 minutes or until potato is tender.

2   Transfer to a food processor or blender with the lime juice and process until smooth. Return to a clean saucepan and reheat for 2-3 minutes. Season to taste with pepper. To serve: spoon into individual bowls.

## SUMMER WHITE GAZPACHO

*A deliciously different approach to the traditional gazpacho that can be prepared in advance for your next dinner party, or served as a refreshing start to a summer meal.*

Serves 6

- ☐ **1 large green bell pepper, seeded and chopped**
- ☐ **1 cucumber, peeled, seeded and chopped**
- ☐ **1 red onion, chopped**
- ☐ **1 cup (125 g) bread crumbs made from stale bread**
- ☐ **³/₄ cup (90 g) ground almonds**
- ☐ **2 cloves garlic, crushed**
- ☐ **3 tablespoons olive oil**
- ☐ **1 teaspoon paprika**
- ☐ **¹/₂ teaspoon sugar**
- ☐ **1 tablespoon white wine vinegar**
- ☐ **3 cups (750 mL) vegetable stock**
- ☐ **ground white pepper**
- ☐ **chopped green bell pepper, chopped cucumber and croutons to garnish**

1   Place pepper, cucumber and onion in food processor or blender and process until smooth. Add bread crumbs, almonds, garlic, oil, paprika, sugar, vinegar and vegetable stock and process until blended. Season to taste with pepper.

2   Transfer to a serving bowl, cover and refrigerate for 2 hours or until well chilled. To serve: Top soup with chopped green pepper, cucumber and croutons.

---

### SOUFFLE COLLARS

To make a paper collar, cut a piece of wax paper 2 inches (5 cm) longer than the circumference of the soufflé dish. Fold in half lengthwise to double the thickness. Wrap it around the soufflé dish; it should extend about 2 inches (5 cm) above the rim of the dish. Secure with string.

---

*Sweet Potato Soup with Ginger and Lime, Summer White Gazpacho, Spinach Timbales with Spicy Pear Sauce*

*While "grazing" is a delightful way to eat – snacking here, tasting there – there is no substitute for sitting down to a hearty main meal with family or friends.*

# MAIN EVENTS
## *with imagination*

---

❖

## CORN ROULADE WITH MUSHROOM FILLING

Serves 4

- ☐ $^1/_4$ **cup (60 g) margarine**
- ☐ **4 tablespoons wholewheat all-purpose plain flour**
- ☐ **6 fl oz (185 mL) milk**
- ☐ **3 eggs, separated**
- ☐ **4 oz (125 g) canned creamed corn**

FILLING

- ☐ **3 fl oz (90 mL) vegetable stock or water**
- ☐ **3 tablespoons dairy sour cream or plain low-fat yogurt**
- ☐ **2 tablespoons chopped fresh basil**
- ☐ **1 tablespoon (15 g) margarine**
- ☐ **6 oz (185 g) mushrooms, finely chopped**
- ☐ **1 onion, finely chopped**
- ☐ **1 tablespoon all-purpose flour**

SAUCE

- ☐ **2 tablespoons (30 g) margarine**
- ☐ **1 onion, chopped**
- ☐ **2 teaspoons all-purpose flour**
- ☐ **1 cup (250 mL) vegetable stock or water**
- ☐ **6$^1/_2$ oz (200 g) canned red peppers, drained and chopped**

1   Melt margarine in a saucepan, stir in flour and cook for 1 minute. Gradually blend in milk and cook over medium heat, stirring frequently, until mixture boils and thickens. Whisk in egg yolks and corn. Whisk egg whites until stiff peaks form and gently fold into corn mixture. Spread mixture into a lightly greased and lined 10 x 12-inch (25 x 30 cm) jelly roll (Swiss roll) pan. Bake at 425°F (220°C) for 15-20 minutes or until puffed and golden.

2   To make filling: Whisk together stock, sour cream and basil. Melt margarine in a saucepan, add mushrooms and onion and cook for 5 minutes or until onion softens. Add flour and cook for 1 minute. Gradually stir in stock mixture and cook over a medium heat, stirring constantly until mixture boils and thickens.

3   To make sauce: Melt margarine in a saucepan and cook onion for 3 minutes, stir in flour and cook for 1 minute longer. Gradually mix in stock and peppers and cook over medium heat, stirring frequently until sauce boils and thickens.

4   Turn roulade onto a wire rack covered with a clean tea-towel and remove paper. Quickly spread with warm filling and gently roll up from the short side, with the help of the tea-towel. Serve roulade sliced with warm sauce.

---

❖

## GINGERED VEGETABLES IN BREAD BASKETS

Serves 4

- ☐ **vegetable oil for deep frying**
- ☐ **2 large pita breads, split through center**

FILLING

- ☐ **8 baby potatoes, cut into bite-size pieces**
- ☐ **1 carrot, peeled and chopped**
- ☐ **1 zucchini, chopped**
- ☐ **8 oz (250 g) snow peas, trimmed**
- ☐ **8 oz (250 g) green and yellow baby squash, trimmed and quartered**
- ☐ **1 tablespoon grated fresh ginger**
- ☐ **2 tablespoons honey**
- ☐ **2 tablespoons orange juice**
- ☐ **2 tablespoons chopped macadamia nuts, toasted**
- ☐ **2 tablespoons finely snipped fresh chives**

1   Heat oil in a wok or large saucepan and cook pita breads one at a time. Press with the head of a metal soup ladle to form a basket. Drain on paper towels. Set aside and keep warm.

2   To make filling: Boil, steam or microwave potatoes, carrot, zucchini, snow peas and squash separately until tender. Set aside and keep warm.

3   Combine ginger, honey, orange juice, nuts and chives in a large bowl. Add vegetables and toss to coat. Spoon filling into warm baskets and serve immediately.

---

❖

## WARM BASIL SUMMER SALAD

*Any small pasta with a good shape for catching the dressing can be used for this salad. You might like to try small shell pasta or small spiral shapes.*

Serves 6

- ☐ **8 oz (250 g) small pasta shapes**
- ☐ **2 tablespoons finely chopped sun-dried tomatoes**
- ☐ **$^1/_2$ red pepper, seeded and thinly sliced**
- ☐ **$^1/_2$ green pepper, seeded and thinly sliced**
- ☐ **2 green onions, chopped**
- ☐ **12 pitted black olives**
- ☐ **2 tablespoons finely chopped basil**
- ☐ **2 tablespoons grated Parmesan cheese**

RED WINE VINEGAR DRESSING

- ☐ **1 clove garlic, crushed**
- ☐ **1 tablespoon olive oil**
- ☐ **3 tablespoons red wine vinegar**
- ☐ **$^1/_4$ teaspoon chili powder**
- ☐ **freshly ground black pepper**

1   Cook pasta in boiling water until al dente. Drain, set aside and keep warm.

2   Place tomatoes, red and green peppers, green onions, olives and basil in a large salad bowl.

3   To make dressing: Place garlic, oil, vinegar and chili powder in a screwtop jar and shake well to combine. Season to taste with pepper.

4   Add warm pasta and dressing to salad bowl and toss lightly to combine. Sprinkle with Parmesan cheese and serve while pasta is still warm.

*Gingered Vegetables in Bread Baskets, Warm Basil Summer Salad, Corn Roulade with Mushroom Filling*

Plates Taitu

## LENTIL WONTONS WITH CILANTRO SAUCE

Makes 40

- ☐ $^1/_2$ oz (15 g) dried mushrooms, soaked in hot water for 10 minutes, drained and finely chopped
- ☐ $3^1/_2$ oz (100 g) fresh spinach, finely chopped
- ☐ 1 tablespoon dry sherry
- ☐ 2 oz (60 g) cabbage, finely chopped
- ☐ 2 teaspoons soy sauce
- ☐ $^1/_2$ teaspoon sesame oil
- ☐ 2 teaspoons grated fresh ginger
- ☐ 4 green onions, finely chopped
- ☐ $^1/_2$ cup (75 g) red lentils, cooked and drained
- ☐ 40 prepared wonton or egg (spring) roll wrappers
- ☐ 1 egg, lightly beaten with $^1/_4$ cup (60 mL) water
- ☐ vegetable oil for deep frying

CILANTRO SAUCE
- ☐ 1 tablespoon vinegar
- ☐ $^1/_3$ cup (100 mL) water
- ☐ 1 teaspoon soy sauce
- ☐ 3 tablespoons honey
- ☐ $^1/_2$ teaspoon sesame oil
- ☐ $^1/_2$ teaspoon grated fresh ginger
- ☐ $^1/_2$ teaspoon sweet chili sauce
- ☐ 2 teaspoons chopped fresh cilantro (coriander) leaves

1   Place mushrooms, spinach, sherry, cabbage, soy sauce, sesame oil, ginger, green onions and lentils in a bowl. Mix well to combine.

2   Place a teaspoon of mixture in the center of each wonton wrapper. Brush the edges with egg mixture and gather up, pressing together firmly.

3   To make sauce: Place vinegar, water, soy sauce, honey, sesame oil, ginger, chili sauce and cilantro in a small saucepan. Cook gently until heated through.

4   Heat oil in a large saucepan and cook wontons for 5 minutes or until golden and crisp. Serve wontons with dipping sauce.

## DOLMAS

Serves 20

- ☐ 12 oz (375 g) preserved grape leaves, rinsed
- ☐ 2 cups (500 mL) vegetable stock or broth, approximately

FILLING
- ☐ 2 oz (60 g) brown rice, cooked
- ☐ 2 oz (60 g) lentils, cooked
- ☐ 2 green onions, chopped
- ☐ 1 small tomato, peeled and chopped
- ☐ 2 tablespoons chopped pine nuts, toasted
- ☐ $^1/_2$ teaspoon grated lemon rind
- ☐ 1 tablespoon lemon juice
- ☐ 2 teaspoons chopped fresh basil
- ☐ 1 clove garlic, crushed
- ☐ 2 teaspoons olive oil

1   Place grape leaves in a saucepan, cover with water and set aside to stand for 5 minutes. Bring to the boil, drain and set aside to cool.

2   To make filling: Place rice, lentils, green onions, tomato, pine nuts, lemon rind, lemon juice, basil, garlic and oil in a bowl and mix well to combine.

3   Place a teaspoon of filling in the center of each leaf and roll up tightly into neat parcels.

4   Place rolls close together in a large heavy-based saucepan or skillet and cover with any remaining grape leaves. Place a plate or saucer over the rolls to prevent them from unrolling during cooking. Pour enough stock over the rolls to cover. Cover, bring to the boil, then reduce heat and simmer for 45 minutes.

> **DID YOU KNOW?**
> The Egyptians left dried beans in the pyramids of the Pharaohs as they believed the beans were helpful in conveying the soul to heaven.

❖

## CURRIED LENTIL AND VEGETABLE SOUP

*A thick and hearty soup to make ahead of time. Great for a main meal!*

Serves 6

- ☐ **2 tablespoons vegetable oil**
- ☐ **1 onion, chopped**
- ☐ **2 teaspoons curry powder**
- ☐ **$^1/_2$ teaspoon ground cumin**
- ☐ **1 tablespoon tomato paste**
- ☐ **6 cups (1.5 litres) vegetable stock or broth**
- ☐ **$^2/_3$ cup (125 g) green or red lentils**
- ☐ **4 oz (125 g) broccoli, broken into small florets**
- ☐ **2 carrots, peeled and chopped**
- ☐ **1 parsnip, peeled and chopped**
- ☐ **1 stalk celery, chopped**
- ☐ **1 tablespoon chopped fresh parsley**

1 Heat oil in a large saucepan and cook onion, curry powder and cumin for 4-5 minutes, or until onion softens. Stir in tomato paste and stock and bring to the boil, stirring occasionally. Reduce heat, add lentils, cover and simmer for 30 minutes.

2 Add broccoli, carrots, parsnip and celery, cover and cook for 30 minutes longer or until vegetables are tender. Stir in parsley just before serving.

*Left: Lentil Wontons with Cilantro Sauce, Dolmas*
*Right: Curried Lentil and Vegetable Soup, Italian-Style Winter Vegetable Soup*

❖

## ITALIAN-STYLE WINTER VEGETABLE SOUP

*A hearty meal in itself that will satisfy even the most hungry members of your family. Delicious with freshly chopped parsley, Parmesan cheese and crusty bread.*

Serves 6

- ☐ **2 tablespoons vegetable oil**
- ☐ **1 large onion, sliced**
- ☐ **1 clove garlic, crushed**
- ☐ **2 stalks celery, chopped**
- ☐ **2 carrots, peeled and chopped**
- ☐ **1 turnip, peeled and chopped**
- ☐ **14 oz (440 g) canned peeled tomatoes, undrained and mashed**
- ☐ **2 tablespoons tomato paste**
- ☐ **1 tablespoon chopped fresh basil**
- ☐ **1 teaspoon dried oregano**
- ☐ **1 teaspoon sugar**
- ☐ **6 cups (1.5 litres) vegetable stock or broth**
- ☐ **4 oz (125 g) small pasta shells**
- ☐ **10 oz (315 g) canned red kidney beans, drained and rinsed**
- ☐ **freshly ground black pepper**

1 Heat oil in a large saucepan and cook onion, garlic, celery, carrots and turnip for 4-5 minutes or until vegetables are just tender.

2 Stir in tomatoes, tomato paste, basil, oregano, sugar and stock. Bring to the boil, reduce heat and simmer for 30-45 minutes.

3 Stir in pasta and beans. Season to taste with pepper and simmer, uncovered, for 30 minutes. To serve, spoon into individual bowls.

Tiles Country Floors China Pillivuyt

## BAKED POTATOES

❖ Baked potatoes are terrific when accompanied with a crisp, green salad. They make a satisfying meal that the whole family will enjoy again and again.

❖ These fillings will be enough to fill six medium potato shells. Just increase or decrease the quantity of filling according to the number of potatoes you wish to fill.

❖ Try these combinations for starters, then be adventurous, and try your own. You will find that there are endless ways to fill a potato!

❖ To cook potatoes, scrub well and bake at 350°F (180°C) for 45 minutes, or microwave on HIGH (100%) for 10 minutes per 16 oz (500 g), or until potatoes are tender.

*Potatoes with tasty fillings from left to right: Curried Cauliflower and Golden Raisins, Mushroom, Sour Cream and Grain Mustard, Asparagus, Avocado and Tarragon, Broiled Pepper, Garlic and Parsley, Spinach and Cheese*

❖

## MUSHROOM, SOUR CREAM AND GRAIN MUSTARD

Serves 6

☐ **6 potatoes, baked in their jackets**

FILLING
☐ **1 tablespoon (15 g) butter**
☐ **4 oz (125 g) button mushrooms, sliced**
☐ **$^{1}/_{2}$ cup (125 g) dairy sour cream**
☐ **2 teaspoons coarse grain mustard**
☐ **2 teaspoons snipped chives**
☐ **$^{1}/_{2}$ cup (60 g) shredded Cheddar cheese**

1 Cut tops from potatoes. Scoop out flesh with a spoon leaving a $^{1}/_{2}$-inch (1 cm) thick shell. Place flesh in a bowl and set aside.

2 To make filling: Melt butter in a saucepan and cook mushrooms for 1-2 minutes. Mash potato flesh with sour cream and mustard. Fold in mushrooms and chives.

3 Spoon mixture into potato shells and sprinkle with cheese. Bake at 350°F (180°C) for 10-15 minutes or until golden.

❖

## ASPARAGUS, AVOCADO AND TARRAGON

Serves 6

☐ **6 potatoes, baked in their jackets**

FILLING
☐ **$9^{1}/_{2}$ oz (300 g) fresh asparagus, cut into 1-inch (2.5 cm) pieces**
☐ **2 tablespoons tarragon vinegar**
☐ **1 teaspoon dried tarragon**
☐ **2 tablespoons lemon juice**
☐ **1 cup (100 g) shredded Cheddar cheese**
☐ **1 avocado, pitted, peeled and cut into 1-inch (2.5 cm) cubes**
☐ **freshly ground black pepper**

1 Cut tops from potatoes. Scoop out flesh with a spoon leaving a $^{1}/_{2}$-inch (1 cm) thick shell. Reserve flesh for other use.

2 To make filling: Boil, steam or microwave asparagus until tender. Combine vinegar, tarragon and lemon juice in a saucepan and boil until reduced by half. Remove from heat and gently stir in asparagus, cheese and avocado. Spoon filling into warmed potato shells, and bake at 350°F (180°C) for 10-15 minutes.

## CURRIED CAULIFLOWER AND GOLDEN RAISINS

Serves 6

☐ 6 potatoes, baked in their jackets

FILLING
☐ 1 tablespoon olive oil
☐ 1/2 teaspoon cumin seeds
☐ 1/2 teaspoon ground coriander
☐ 1 small red chili, finely chopped
☐ 1/4 teaspoon ground turmeric
☐ 5 oz (155 g) cauliflower, cut into small florets
☐ 1/3 cup (60 g) golden raisins
☐ 1/3 cup (90 g) plain yogurt

1   Cut tops from potatoes. Scoop out flesh with a spoon leaving a 1/2-inch (1 cm) thick shell. Reserve flesh and place in a mixing bowl. Keep shells warm.
2   To make filling: Heat oil in a skillet and cook cumin, coriander, chili and turmeric for 1 minute. Add cauliflower, toss to coat with spice mixture and cook for 6-8 minutes or until tender. Mash potato flesh. Combine potato, raisins and yogurt with cauliflower mixture. Spoon into the potato shells and serve.

## SPINACH AND CHEESE

Serves 6

☐ 6 potatoes, baked in their jackets

FILLING
☐ 1 tablespoon olive oil
☐ 1 onion, thinly sliced
☐ 6 large spinach leaves, stalks removed and leaves finely shredded
☐ 3 hard-cooked eggs, finely chopped
☐ 1/2 cup (60 g) blue cheese, crumbled
☐ 4 tablespoons dairy sour cream
☐ freshly ground black pepper

1   Cut tops from potatoes. Scoop out flesh with a spoon leaving a 1/2-inch (1 cm) thick shell. Reserve flesh for another use and keep shells warm.
2   To make filling: Heat oil in a skillet and cook onion until crisp and golden. Drain on paper towels. Combine onion, spinach and eggs. Set aside.
3   Combine blue cheese and sour cream in a mixing bowl and beat until smooth and slightly runny. Season to taste with pepper.
4   Fill potato shells with spinach mixture. Top with blue cheese mixture and serve.

## BROILED PEPPER, GARLIC AND PARSLEY

Serves 6

☐ 6 potatoes, baked in their jackets

FILLING
☐ 2 red peppers, cut into quarters
☐ 1 green pepper, cut into quarters
☐ 2 cloves garlic, crushed
☐ 2 teaspoons olive oil
☐ 2 tablespoons chopped fresh flat leaf parsley
☐ 2 tablespoons shredded mozzarella cheese

1   Cut tops from potatoes. Scoop out flesh with a spoon leaving a 1/2-inch (1 cm) thick shell. Place flesh in a bowl and set aside.
2   Broil red and green peppers until skin blisters. Peel and slice thinly. Mash potato flesh with garlic, oil and parsley. Fold through peppers and spoon into potato shells. Sprinkle with mozzarella and bake at 350°F (180°C) for 10 minutes or until cheese melts and is golden.

## SUMMER FRITTATA

Serves 6

- ☐ **2 tablespoons (30 g) margarine**
- ☐ **1 clove garlic, crushed**
- ☐ **4 zucchini, sliced**
- ☐ **8 eggs, lightly beaten**
- ☐ **2 tablespoons chopped sun-dried tomatoes**
- ☐ **6 green onions, finely chopped**
- ☐ **1 tablespoon chopped fresh basil**
- ☐ **1 tablespoon chopped fresh mint**
- ☐ **freshly ground black pepper**
- ☐ **¼ cup (30 g) shredded Cheddar cheese**

1 Melt margarine in a large skillet and cook garlic and zucchini over medium heat for 5-6 minutes, or until zucchini are just tender.

2 Place eggs, tomatoes, green onions, basil and mint in a bowl and mix to combine. Season to taste with pepper. Pour over zucchini in pan and gently move vegetables to allow the egg mixture to run under. Reduce heat to low and cook until frittata is brown on the bottom and just set.

3 Slide onto a cookie sheet, sprinkle with cheese and place under a preheated broiler for 4-5 minutes or until cheese melts and is golden. Serve hot, warm or at room temperature, cut into wedges.

❖

## RISOTTO PRIMAVERA

Serves 8

- ☐ **13 oz (410 g) yellow baby squash, cut into quarters**
- ☐ **4 zucchini, thickly sliced**
- ☐ **2 red peppers, seeded and cut into quarters**
- ☐ **8 oz (250 g) fresh asparagus cut into 1-inch (2.5 cm) pieces**
- ☐ **freshly ground black pepper**
- ☐ **3 tablespoons grated fresh Parmesan cheese**

RISOTTO

- ☐ **½ cup (1 stick/125 g) butter**
- ☐ **2 leeks, sliced**
- ☐ **2 cloves garlic, crushed**
- ☐ **16 oz (500 g) Arborio rice**
- ☐ **1 cup (250 mL) dry white wine**
- ☐ **3 tablespoons tarragon vinegar**
- ☐ **2 bay leaves**
- ☐ **3 cups (750 mL) vegetable stock or broth**
- ☐ **6 sun-dried tomatoes, chopped**
- ☐ **1 tablespoon chopped fresh basil**
- ☐ **freshly ground black pepper**

1 To make risotto: Melt butter in a heavy saucepan and cook leeks and garlic until soft and transparent. Stir in rice, tossing well to coat with butter.

2 Stir in wine and vinegar and simmer until most of liquid is absorbed. Add bay leaves and 2 cups (500 mL) stock or broth. Simmer until liquid is absorbed. Stir in sun-dried tomatoes and remaining stock. Simmer, stirring frequently, until liquid is almost absorbed and rice is tender. Remove bay leaves. Stir in basil and pepper to taste.

3 Boil, steam or microwave squash, zucchini and asparagus separately until tender. Set aside and keep warm. Broil peppers, skin-side up, until skin blisters. Peel and slice thickly. Toss vegetables together and season to taste with black pepper. To serve: Place risotto on a serving platter and surround with vegetables. Sprinkle with Parmesan cheese.

*Cheese and Onion Bread Pudding,*
*Risotto Primavera*

Plates Villeroy & Boch *Dish Pillivuyt*

## CHEESY TOFU AND VEGETABLE STRUDEL

Serves 6

- [ ] **12 sheets filo pastry**
- [ ] **3 tablespoons (45 g) margarine, melted**
- [ ] **2 teaspoons grated Parmesan cheese**
- [ ] **2 teaspoons sesame seeds**

FILLING
- [ ] **6¹/₂ oz (200 g) fresh asparagus, chopped**
- [ ] **2 carrots, peeled and shredded**
- [ ] **2 potatoes, shredded**
- [ ] **3 tablespoons tomato paste**
- [ ] **11 oz (350 g) firm tofu, cut into ¹/₂-inch (1 cm) cubes**
- [ ] **3 tablespoons chopped fresh basil**
- [ ] **1 cup (100 g) shredded Cheddar cheese**
- [ ] **3 tablespoons dairy sour cream**
- [ ] **freshly ground black pepper**

1   To make filling: Boil, steam or microwave asparagus, carrots and potatoes separately until just tender. Drain. Place cooked vegetables, tomato paste, tofu, basil, cheese and sour cream in a bowl and mix well to combine. Season to taste with pepper. Divide mixture in half.

2   Layer 6 pastry sheets, brushing each sheet with melted margarine. Spoon one half of vegetable mixture along one long edge of pastry, leaving a 3-inch (7.5 cm) border, fold in edges and roll up carefully like a jelly (Swiss) roll. Repeat with remaining pastry and mixture.

3   Carefully lift strudels onto a lightly greased cookie sheet, brush top with any remaining margarine and sprinkle with Parmesan cheese and sesame seeds. Bake at 350°F (180°C) for 25 minutes or until golden.

## CHEESE AND ONION BREAD PUDDING

Serves 6

- [ ] **2 tablespoons (30 g) margarine**
- [ ] **3 large onions, thinly sliced**
- [ ] **¹/₂ teaspoon dried thyme**
- [ ] **¹/₂ cup (60 g) grated Parmesan cheese**
- [ ] **¹/₂ cup (60 g) shredded smoked cheese**
- [ ] **1 cup (125 g) shredded Cheddar cheese**
- [ ] **1 tablespoon snipped fresh chives**
- [ ] **8 slices wholewheat bread, crusts removed**
- [ ] **3 eggs, lightly beaten**
- [ ] **2 cups (500 mL) milk**
- [ ] **freshly ground black pepper**

1   Heat margarine in a skillet and cook onions and thyme over a gentle heat for 10-15 minutes, or until onions are golden and soft.

2   Combine Parmesan, smoked and Cheddar cheeses and chives. Place half the bread slices in a greased baking dish, cutting slices to fit snugly, if necessary. Cover with onion mixture and sprinkle with half the cheese mixture. Repeat with remaining bread and cheese.

3   Place eggs and milk in a bowl and whisk to combine. Season to taste with pepper. Pour over bread and cheese in baking dish and bake at 375°F (190°C) for 30-35 minutes, or until custard is firm and golden.

*Cheesy Tofu and Vegetable Strudel, Summer Frittata*

## SWEET AND SOUR RICE BALLS

Makes 16

- ☐ **2 tablespoons (30 g) margarine**
- ☐ **10 oz (315 g) short-grain rice**
- ☐ **4 green onions, finely chopped**
- ☐ **2 teaspoons grated fresh ginger**
- ☐ **3 cups (750 mL) vegetable stock or broth**
- ☐ **1¼ cups (155 g) shredded Cheddar cheese**
- ☐ **1 egg, lightly beaten**
- ☐ **all-purpose flour**
- ☐ **1 egg, beaten with ¼ cup (60 mL) milk**
- ☐ **¾ cup (200 g) wholewheat bread crumbs made from stale bread**
- ☐ **vegetable oil for deep frying**

SWEET AND SOUR SAUCE
- ☐ **4 dried mushrooms, soaked in hot water for 10 minutes, drained and finely chopped**
- ☐ **7 oz (220 g) canned pineapple chunks, chopped and juice reserved**
- ☐ **4 green onions, finely chopped**
- ☐ **2 teaspoons hoisin sauce**
- ☐ **1 tablespoon vinegar**
- ☐ **1 cup (250 mL) water blended with 1 tablespoon cornstarch**
- ☐ **1 teaspoon sambal oelek (prepared chopped hot red chilies)**
- ☐ **2 teaspoons soy sauce**
- ☐ **2 teaspoons tamarind paste**

1 Melt margarine in a saucepan, stir in rice, green onions and ginger and cook, stirring frequently, for 2 minutes. Pour in vegetable stock or broth and bring to the boil, stirring occasionally. Reduce heat, cover with a tight-fitting lid and simmer for 20 minutes, or until rice is tender and liquid absorbed. Remove from heat and set aside to cool. Mix in cheese and egg.
2 Spread mixture in a lightly oiled 8 x 12-inch (20 x 30 cm) shallow pan, cover and refrigerate until firm.
3 To make sauce: Combine mushrooms, pineapple, ¼ cup (60 mL) reserved pineapple juice, green onions, hoisin sauce, vinegar, cornstarch mixture, sambal oelek, soy sauce and tamarind paste in a saucepan. Cook over medium heat until mixture boils and thickens.
4 Divide rice mixture into sixteen portions and roll into balls. Toss balls in flour, dip in egg mixture and roll in bread crumbs.
5 Heat oil in a large saucepan and cook a few balls at a time for 3-4 minutes or until golden. Drain on paper towels and serve with sauce.

---

### DID YOU KNOW?
Polenta was the food of the Roman soldiers. It is one of the many Italian dishes that date back to antiquity, and was originally made with millet and wheat. This simple peasant food is now very popular and the perfect foil for spicy dishes.

---

## POLENTA CROQUETTES WITH TOMATO SAUCE

*The sharp tang of chilies combines well with mint in this tomato-based sauce.*

Makes 12

- ☐ **4 cups (1 litre) vegetable stock, broth or water**
- ☐ **6½ oz (200 g) polenta**
- ☐ **4 green onions, finely chopped**
- ☐ **1 stalk celery, finely chopped**
- ☐ **½ small red pepper, finely chopped**
- ☐ **all-purpose flour**
- ☐ **2 eggs, lightly beaten with ½ cup (125 mL) milk**
- ☐ **⅔ cup (200 g) wholewheat bread crumbs made from stale bread mixed with 1 teaspoon ground cumin**
- ☐ **vegetable oil for shallow frying**

TOMATO SAUCE
- ☐ **14 oz (440 g) canned peeled tomatoes, undrained and mashed**
- ☐ **2 tablespoons finely chopped fresh mint**
- ☐ **2 teaspoons curry powder**
- ☐ **2 small red chilies, finely chopped**

1 Place vegetable stock or broth in a large saucepan and bring to the boil, then stir in polenta. Cover and simmer for 30 minutes or until thick. Add green onions, celery and pepper and mix well. Spread into a lightly greased 8 x 12-inch (20 x 30 cm) shallow pan (tin). Set aside to stand for 2 hours.
2 Cut polenta into fingers, toss in flour, dip in egg mixture and then in bread crumb mixture. Refrigerate for 15 minutes or until required.
3 To make sauce: Combine tomatoes, mint, curry powder and chilies in a saucepan. Bring to the boil and cook stirring for 5 minutes or until sauce thickens.
4 Heat oil in a large saucepan and cook polenta fingers a few at a time for 3-4 minutes or until golden. Drain on paper towels and serve with sauce.

---

## THAI-STYLE VEGETARIAN CURRY

*A spicy, fragrant curry – delicious when served with jasmine or saffron-flavored rice.*

Serves 6

- ☐ **2 tablespoons peanut oil**
- ☐ **2 onions, sliced**
- ☐ **2 cloves garlic, crushed**
- ☐ **2 small red chilies, finely chopped**
- ☐ **2 teaspoons grated fresh ginger**
- ☐ **2 tablespoons chopped cilantro (fresh coriander) leaves**
- ☐ **1 teaspoon ground cumin**
- ☐ **1 tablespoon red curry paste**
- ☐ **1 small head cauliflower, cut into florets**
- ☐ **3 large potatoes, peeled and roughly chopped**
- ☐ **1 eggplant, cut into 1-inch (2.5 cm) pieces**
- ☐ **2 carrots, peeled and thickly sliced**
- ☐ **4 zucchini, roughly chopped**
- ☐ **3 tablespoons fish sauce**
- ☐ **14 oz (440 g) canned coconut cream**
- ☐ **2 tablespoons chopped fresh basil**
- ☐ **1 teaspoon grated lime rind**

1 Heat oil in a saucepan and cook onions, garlic, chilies, ginger, cilantro and cumin for 5 minutes, or until onions soften. Stir in curry paste, cauliflower, potatoes, eggplant and carrots, and cook for 2-3 minutes longer. Toss vegetables to coat with spices.
2 Mix in zucchini, fish sauce, coconut cream, basil and lime rind, cover and simmer, stirring occasionally, for 15 minutes, or until vegetables are tender and sauce thickens slightly.

*From left: Sweet and Sour Rice Balls, Polenta Croquettes with Tomato Sauce, Savory Squash Tart, Thai-Style Vegetarian Curry, Spinach Timbales with Pasta Filling*

❖
## SAVORY SQUASH TART

Serves 4

- ☐ **4 sheets filo pastry**
- ☐ **2 tablespoons vegetable oil**
- ☐ **1 onion, chopped**
- ☐ **8 oz (250 g) butternut squash, peeled, seeded, cooked and mashed**
- ☐ **1¹/₂ cups (185 g) shredded Cheddar cheese**
- ☐ **2 eggs, separated**
- ☐ **2 tablespoons dairy sour cream or plain low-fat yogurt**
- ☐ **freshly ground black pepper**
- ☐ **pinch chili powder**
- ☐ **1 tablespoon chopped fresh parsley**

1   Brush each sheet of pastry with oil and fold in half. Layer pastry, one folded piece on top of the other, to give eight layers. Place a 7-inch (18 cm) tart pan upside down on the layered pastry and cut around dish making a circle 2 inches (5 cm) larger. Lift all layers of pastry into tart pan and roll down edges.

2   Heat remaining oil in a skillet and cook onion for 3-4 minutes or until soft. Combine onion, squash, cheese, egg yolks and sour cream. Season to taste with pepper and chili powder.

3   Whisk egg whites until stiff peaks form. Fold into squash mixture and spoon into pastry shell. Sprinkle with parsley. Bake at 400°F (200°C) for 30 minutes.

❖
## SPINACH TIMBALES WITH PASTA FILLING

Serves 4

- ☐ **6 large spinach leaves, washed and stalks removed**

FILLING
- ☐ **2 tablespoons olive oil**
- ☐ **2 small eggplants, chopped**
- ☐ **1 onion, chopped**
- ☐ **1 clove garlic, crushed**
- ☐ **1 red pepper, chopped**
- ☐ **2 zucchini, chopped**
- ☐ **1 large ripe tomato, peeled and chopped**
- ☐ **2 tablespoons tomato paste**
- ☐ **1 teaspoon hot chili powder**
- ☐ **3 tablespoons finely chopped pitted black olives**
- ☐ **4 tablespoons risoni (rice shaped) pasta, cooked**
- ☐ **3 tablespoons grated Parmesan cheese**
- ☐ **freshly ground black pepper**

1   Boil, steam or microwave spinach until wilted. Drain well. Line four greased individual soufflé cups (1 cup/250 mL capacity) with spinach. Allow some leaves to overhang top.

2   To make filling: Heat oil in a saucepan and cook eggplants, onion, garlic, pepper, zucchini and tomato, stirring occasionally, for 15 minutes or until mixture thickens. Add tomato paste, chili powder, olives, pasta and Parmesan cheese. Season to taste with pepper and mix well to combine.

3   Spoon filling into lined soufflé cups, fold overhanging leaves over filling and cover with greased aluminum foil. Bake at 350°F (180°C) for 20 minutes. Allow to stand for 5-10 minutes before turning out.

---

### NUTRITION TIP

When compared by weight, the vegetable which is lowest in calories (kilojoules) is celery, followed closely by lettuce and cucumber. Three stalks of celery, 20 lettuce leaves or ¹/₂ cucumber contain the same calories (kilojoules) as half a slice of bread.

## TOFU AND PEANUT BURGERS

Serves 6

- [ ] **6 wholegrain rolls, split and toasted**
- [ ] **6 lettuce leaves**
- [ ] **6 slices cooked beets**
- [ ] **2 hard-cooked eggs, chopped**
- [ ] **1/4 cup (60 g) dairy sour cream**

TOFU AND NUT PATTIES
- [ ] **8 oz (250 g) firm tofu, drained**
- [ ] **2 carrots, peeled, shredded and squeezed of excess liquid**
- [ ] **2 zucchini, shredded and squeezed of excess liquid**
- [ ] **1/3 cup (60 g) unsalted, roasted peanuts, finely chopped**
- [ ] **2/3 cup (60 g) walnuts, finely chopped**
- [ ] **4 oz (125 g) wholewheat bread crumbs made from stale bread**
- [ ] **1/2 teaspoon ground fenugreek**
- [ ] **1 teaspoon ground coriander**
- [ ] **freshly ground black pepper**
- [ ] **2 tablespoons sesame seeds**
- [ ] **2 tablespoons poppy seeds**
- [ ] **2 tablespoons vegetable oil**

1   To make patties: Mash tofu in a large bowl. Stir in carrots, zucchini, peanuts, walnuts, bread crumbs, fenugreek and coriander. Season to taste with pepper. Combine sesame and poppy seeds. Shape mixture into six patties and roll in seeds.

2   Heat oil in a skillet and cook patties for 4-5 minutes on each side, or until crisp and golden brown.

3   Line bottom of each roll with a lettuce leaf, then top with a pattie, beet slice, spoonful of egg and a spoonful of sour cream. Replace top of roll and serve.

❖

## TASTY FILO TRIANGLES

Makes 30

- [ ] **18 sheets filo pastry**
- [ ] **3 oz (90 g) polyunsaturated margarine, melted**
- [ ] **2 tablespoons grated Parmesan cheese**

FILLING
- [ ] **10 oz (315 g) yellow split peas**
- [ ] **1 tablespoon olive oil**
- [ ] **1/2 teaspoon ground cumin**
- [ ] **1/4 teaspoon ground coriander**
- [ ] **1 clove garlic, crushed**
- [ ] **2 teaspoons grated fresh ginger**
- [ ] **1 small fresh red chili, finely chopped**
- [ ] **2 tablespoons tomato paste**
- [ ] **1 teaspoon grated lemon rind**
- [ ] **10 oz (315 g) mushrooms, finely chopped**
- [ ] **8 oz (250 g) cottage cheese**
- [ ] **2 tablespoons snipped fresh chives**
- [ ] **freshly ground black pepper**

1   To make filling: Cover peas with water and set aside to stand overnight. Drain and rinse well. Place peas in a saucepan of boiling water and cook for 20 minutes or until soft. Drain and set aside to cool.

2   Heat oil in a saucepan and cook cumin, coriander, garlic, ginger, chili, tomato paste and lemon rind for 1-2 minutes. Add peas and mushrooms and cook, stirring frequently, for 10 minutes, or until most of the liquid has evaporated. Stir in cottage cheese and chives. Season with pepper.

3   Layer 3 pastry sheets together, brushing each sheet with margarine. Cut pastry crosswise into six equal strips. Place a teaspoon of pea mixture on one end of each strip. Fold corner of pastry over filling to form a triangle shape. Lift first triangle up and over and continue folding to end of strip. Repeat with remaining pastry, margarine and pea mixture.

4   Place triangles on a cookie sheet, brush with remaining margarine and sprinkle with Parmesan cheese. Bake at 425°F (220°C) for 15 minutes or until golden.

❖

## MARINATED TOFU AND VEGETABLE SATAYS

*Great for a vegetarian barbecue.*

Serves 6

- [ ] **8 oz (250 g) button mushrooms**
- [ ] **12 pickling onions (whole baby white)**
- [ ] **2 green peppers, seeded and cut into pieces**
- [ ] **12 baby yellow (patty pan) squash**
- [ ] **2 red peppers, seeded and cut into pieces**
- [ ] **1 eggplant, cut into cubes**
- [ ] **8 oz (250 g) firm tofu, cut into cubes**

MARINADE
- [ ] **1/2 cup (125 mL) soy sauce**
- [ ] **1/4 cup (60 mL) dry sherry**
- [ ] **2 tablespoons honey**

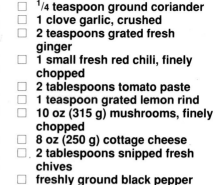

*Plates Taitu*

*Plates Limoges*

## SATAY SAUCE

- ☐ ³/₄ cup (220 g) crunchy peanut butter
- ☐ 1 small red chili, finely chopped
- ☐ 2 cloves garlic, crushed
- ☐ ³/₄ cup (220 mL) water
- ☐ 1 tablespoon packed brown sugar
- ☐ 2 teaspoons soy sauce
- ☐ 1 tablespoon lemon juice

1　To make marinade: Combine soy sauce, sherry and honey in a shallow dish. Thread mushrooms, onions, green pepper, squash, red pepper, eggplant and tofu onto twelve greased wooden skewers and place in marinade. Cover and set aside for 30 minutes, turning once.

2　Remove skewers from marinade and cook under a preheated broiler, or on a barbecue, for 10 minutes or until vegetables are tender. Brush frequently with marinade during cooking.

3　To make sauce: Combine peanut butter, chili, garlic, water, sugar, soy sauce and lemon juice in a saucepan and cook over low heat for 10 minutes. If sauce becomes too thick add a little more water or lemon juice. Spoon sauce over skewers and serve immediately.

❖

# CHEESY MUSHROOM AND ZUCCHINI BAKE

*Served with a crisp, garden salad for a tasty meal, this simply prepared dish has a crunchy, sesame seed topping.*

Serves 6

- ☐ ¹/₄ cup (¹/₂ stick/60 g) butter
- ☐ 2 onions, roughly chopped
- ☐ 2 cloves garlic, crushed
- ☐ 1 carrot, peeled and shredded
- ☐ 3 zucchini, shredded
- ☐ 10 oz (315 g) mushrooms, sliced
- ☐ 3 eggs, lightly beaten
- ☐ 2 tablespoons all-purpose flour
- ☐ 2 tablespoons chopped fresh parsley
- ☐ ¹/₂ cup (60 g) shredded Cheddar cheese
- ☐ freshly ground black pepper

TOPPING
- ☐ ¹/₂ cup (60 g) shredded Cheddar cheese
- ☐ 1 tablespoon sesame seeds

1　Melt butter in a saucepan and cook onions and garlic for 2-3 minutes or until onions are soft. In a large bowl, combine onion mixture, carrot, zucchini, mushrooms, eggs, flour, parsley and cheese. Season to taste with pepper. Spoon mixture into a lightly greased 7-inch (18 cm) springform pan.

2　To make topping: Combine cheese and sesame seeds. Sprinkle over vegetable mixture. Bake at 350°F (180°C) for 30 minutes until firm. Allow to stand 5-10 minutes before removing from pan.

---

### DID YOU KNOW?

Battle Creek, Michigan, USA was where breakfast cereals, peanut butter and vegetable protein foods all originated. The development of these foods goes back to Dr. John Harvey Kellogg who was the medical director of the Seventh Day Adventist Health Reform Institute, later to be known as Battle Creek Sanitarium.

---

*Left: Tofu and Peanut Burgers*
*Above: Tasty Filo Triangles, Cheesy Mushroom and Zucchini Bake, Marinated Tofu and Vegetable Satays*

*You walk in late, and everyone is waiting for dinner. What to cook? In this section you will find delicious recipes that can be whipped up in minutes.*

# HOME LATE
## *dinner can't wait*

❖

## VEGETABLE AND NUT STIR-FRY

Serves 6

- ☐ **2 tablespoons vegetable oil**
- ☐ **2 onions, cut into eighths**
- ☐ **2 carrots, peeled and cut into thin strips**
- ☐ **2 stalks celery, cut into thin strips**
- ☐ **2 teaspoons turmeric**
- ☐ **2 cloves garlic, crushed**
- ☐ **6 green onions, chopped**
- ☐ **2 tablespoons vinegar**
- ☐ **2 tablespoons sugar**
- ☐ **1 mango, pitted, peeled and chopped**
- ☐ **4 oz (125 g) snow peas, trimmed**
- ☐ **³/₄ cup (185 mL) vegetable stock or broth**
- ☐ **4 oz (125 g) roasted cashew nuts**

1   Heat oil in a wok or skillet. Add onions, carrots and celery and stir-fry for 5 minutes or until lightly browned. Combine turmeric, garlic, green onions, vinegar and sugar and stir into wok.
2   Add mango, snow peas and stock or broth, and stir-fry for 5 minutes, or until vegetables are just tender. Fold in nuts and serve immediately.

---

### BALSAMIC VINEGAR

Balsamic vinegar is a dark Italian vinegar made by the special processing of wines and musts from the Modena province. It is an interesting addition to any salad dressing, and can also be used in sauces for meats or vegetables. Balsamic vinegar is available from delicatessens and some supermarkets.

❖

## WARM RED CABBAGE SALAD

*Make this wonderful warm salad in autumn when apples and red cabbage are plentiful and at their best.*

Serves 6

- ☐ **1 tablespoon olive oil**
- ☐ **1 clove garlic, crushed**
- ☐ **1 red onion, thinly sliced**
- ☐ **2 tablespoons balsamic vinegar**
- ☐ **¹/₂ small head red cabbage, shredded**
- ☐ **2 green apples, peeled, cored and thinly sliced**
- ☐ **1 tablespoon finely snipped fresh chives**
- ☐ **1 tablespoon finely chopped fresh dill**
- ☐ **¹/₂ cup (60 g) slivered almonds, toasted**
- ☐ **¹/₂ cup (60 g) feta cheese, crumbled**

1   Heat oil in a large skillet. Add garlic and onion and cook over medium heat for 2-3 minutes. Stir in vinegar and cook for 1 minute longer.
2   Add cabbage to pan, toss lightly and cook for 4-5 minutes or until cabbage just starts to wilt and change color. Transfer cabbage mixture to a salad bowl. Toss in apples, chives and dill. Sprinkle top of the salad with almonds and cheese and serve while salad is still warm.

*Warm Red Cabbage Salad, Blue Cheese and Apple Omelet, Vegetable and Nut Stir-Fry*

Plates Made in Japan

❖

## BLUE CHEESE AND APPLE OMELET

*Cheese and apples are natural partners, but as a filling in this omelet, they are an extra-special combination.*

Serves 1

☐ **1 tablespoon (15 g) margarine**
☐ **2 eggs**
☐ **2 teaspoons water**
☐ **freshly ground black pepper**

FILLING
☐ **1 tablespoon (15 g) margarine**
☐ **$^1/_2$ small green apple, cored and thinly sliced**
☐ **1 oz (30 g) blue cheese, crumbled**
☐ **1 teaspoon finely snipped chives**

1 To make filling: Melt margarine in a small skillet and cook apple over low heat for 2-3 minutes or until just heated through. Remove from pan and set aside to keep warm.

2 To make omelet: Melt margarine in a small skillet or omelet pan. Lightly whisk together eggs and water. Season to taste with pepper and pour into pan. Cook over medium heat, continually drawing in the edge of the omelet with a fork during cooking, until no liquid remains and the omelet is lightly set.

3 Top omelet with apple slices, blue cheese and chives and fold in half. Slide onto a plate and serve immediately.

## RICE FRITTERS

*Serve with hummus or minted yogurt.*

Makes 20

- ☐ ¼ teaspoon chili powder
- ☐ 1 teaspoon garam masala
- ☐ 2½ oz (75 g) wholewheat all-purpose flour
- ☐ 2½ oz (75 g) besan flour
- ☐ 4 oz (125 g) brown rice, cooked
- ☐ 2 eggs, lightly beaten with ¾ cup (185 mL) milk
- ☐ 4 green onions, finely chopped
- ☐ ½ small red pepper, seeded and finely chopped
- ☐ vegetable oil for shallow frying

1   Sift chili powder, garam masala and wholewheat and besan flours into a bowl. Mix in rice, make a well in the center and gradually stir in egg mixture. Mix to a smooth batter and stir in green onions and pepper.

2   Heat oil in a skillet and cook spoonfuls of batter for 3-4 minutes or until golden each side. Drain on paper towels and serve.

## RAINBOW FRITTATA WITH COCONUT CREAM

Serves 6

- ☐ 3½ oz (100 g) dried yellow mung beans, soaked In water overnight
- ☐ 2 eggs
- ☐ 2 tablespoons vegetable oil
- ☐ 1 onion, sliced
- ☐ 2 potatoes, peeled and shredded
- ☐ 2 carrots, peeled and shredded
- ☐ 2 zucchini, shredded
- ☐ 4 oz (125 g) canned corn kernels, drained
- ☐ 3 tablespoons chopped fresh basil
- ☐ freshly ground black pepper
- ☐ ¾ cup (100 g) shredded Cheddar cheese

### COCONUT CREAM
- ☐ ½ cup (125 mL) coconut cream
- ☐ 1 tablespoon lemon juice
- ☐ 2 tablespoons chopped fresh mint

1   Drain mung beans and place in food processor or blender with eggs and process until smooth. Place mung bean mixture in a large mixing bowl.

2   Heat 1 tablespoon oil in a skillet and cook onion gently for 3-4 minutes. Add potatoes, carrots and zucchini and cook, stirring for 5 minutes or until vegetables soften. Remove from pan and pat dry with paper towels. Combine cooked vegetables, bean mixture, corn kernels and basil. Mix and season to taste with pepper.

2   Heat remaining oil in a large skillet, add vegetable mixture and sprinkle with cheese. Cook over low heat for 5-8 minutes or until just firm, shaking pan occasionally so that the frittata does not stick. Place pan under a preheated broiler for 3 minutes, or until the frittata is browned on the top.

3   To make cream: Place coconut cream, lemon juice and mint in a screwtop jar and shake well to combine. Invert frittata onto a plate, cut into wedges and serve with Coconut Cream.

---

### BESAN FLOUR
Besan flour is flour made from chickpeas and can be found at Asian specialty food stores.

*Plates Villeroy & Boch*

## STIR-FRIED VEGETABLES WITH EGGS

*Often called Egg Foo Yung and traditionally made with shrimp, fish or beef, this popular recipe is delicious just made with vegetables.*

Serves 2

- ☐ **4 oz (125 g) snow peas, trimmed**
- ☐ **6 oz (185 g) fresh asparagus, cut into 2-inch (5 cm) pieces**
- ☐ **3 eggs**
- ☐ **1 teaspoon sesame oil**
- ☐ **3 tablespoons water**
- ☐ **1 teaspoon dry sherry**
- ☐ **1 teaspoon soy sauce**
- ☐ **freshly ground black pepper**
- ☐ **1 tablespoon vegetable oil**
- ☐ **3 green onions, chopped**

1  Boil, steam or microwave snow peas and asparagus separately until just tender. Drain. Refresh under cold running water. Drain well and set aside.

2  Place eggs, sesame oil, water, sherry and soy sauce in a bowl and whisk lightly to combine. Season to taste with pepper.

3  Heat oil in a wok or skillet, add egg mixture and stir-fry for 1 minute, or until egg just begins to set. Add snow peas, asparagus and green onions, and stir-fry for 1 minute longer. Serve immediately.

## INDIAN EGG CURRY

*A delicious egg curry that combines all the tastes of India.*

Serves 6

- ☐ **6 hard-cooked eggs, halved lengthwise**

SAUCE

- ☐ **1 tablespoon vegetable oil**
- ☐ **1 large onion, finely chopped**
- ☐ **1 clove garlic, crushed**
- ☐ **1 tablespoon finely chopped fresh ginger**
- ☐ **1 teaspoon ground cumin**
- ☐ **1 teaspoon ground coriander**
- ☐ **1/2 teaspoon chili powder**
- ☐ **1 teaspoon ground turmeric**
- ☐ **14 oz (440 g) canned tomatoes, undrained and mashed**
- ☐ **1/2 cup (125 mL) coconut milk**
- ☐ **freshly ground black pepper**

1  To make sauce: Heat oil in a skillet and cook onion, garlic and ginger over medium heat for 5 minutes or until onion softens. Stir in cumin, coriander, chili powder and turmeric, and cook for 2 minutes longer.

2  Add tomatoes and coconut milk, bring to the boil, then reduce heat and simmer for 15 minutes or until reduced to a thick sauce. Season to taste with pepper.

3  Place eggs in a shallow baking dish and spoon sauce over. Cover and bake at 350°F (180°C) for 20 minutes or until heated through.

---

### BOILING EGGS

✧  Hard-cooked eggs that are very fresh can be difficult to peel. Try peeling them under cold water.

✧  To prevent a grey-green ring forming around the yolk, take care not to overcook your eggs, and cool cooked eggs immediately in cold running water.

---

*Left: Rainbow Frittata with Coconut Cream, Rice Fritters*
*Above: Indian Egg Curry, Stir-Fried Vegetables with Eggs*

## SPINACH PIE

*Serve this quick-to-make pie hot or cold. Any leftovers are great to put in school or office lunch boxes.*

Serves 8

- [ ] **8 large spinach leaves, stems removed and leaves shredded**
- [ ] **2 tablespoons (30 g) butter**
- [ ] **1 onion, finely chopped**
- [ ] **1 cup (125 g) ricotta cheese**
- [ ] **1 cup (125 g) feta cheese, crumbled**
- [ ] **¹/₂ cup (60 g) shredded Cheddar cheese**
- [ ] **3 tablespoons grated Parmesan cheese**
- [ ] **4 eggs, lightly beaten**
- [ ] **¹/₄ teaspoon ground nutmeg**
- [ ] **freshly ground black pepper**
- [ ] **8 sheets filo pastry**
- [ ] **3 tablespoons olive oil**

1   Boil, steam or microwave spinach until just tender. Drain and cool completely, then squeeze to remove excess liquid. Chop spinach finely and place in a bowl.
2   Melt butter in a skillet and cook onion for 4-5 minutes or until golden. Combine onion, spinach, ricotta, feta, Cheddar and Parmesan cheeses. Mix together eggs, nutmeg and pepper to taste, then fold into spinach mixture.
3   Layer 4 sheets of pastry together, brushing between each sheet with oil. Repeat with remaining sheets. Line a deep lightly greased baking dish with a pastry layer. Trim edges with scissors about 1 inch (2.5 cm) from the edge of dish. Spoon in spinach filling, then fold remaining pastry layer in half and place on top of spinach filling. Gently fold edges of pastry together, brush top with oil and bake at 400°F (200°C) for 40-45 minutes or until golden and crisp.

---

### DID YOU KNOW?

Legumes are dried beans, pulses and lentils. They are frequently eaten as canned baked beans, but they form an important part of the diet of many other cultures. They are an excellent source of protein, iron and fiber and are inexpensive to buy. Their fiber is the soluble type which can lower blood cholesterol and control glucose levels in diabetics. Although dried beans are time consuming to prepare, they can be soaked and precooked in large quantities, and then frozen in meal-sized servings for later use.

---

### VEGETABLE TIPS

❖  Wash vegetables before preparing, but do not soak. Soaking tends to draw out the valuable water soluble vitamins resulting in vegetables with a lower nutrient content.

As with every rule there are always exceptions and it may be necessary to soak very dirty vegetables to remove dirt. In these cases always keep soaking times to a minimum.

Many of the precious vitamins and minerals found in vegetables are stored just under their skin. Only peel vegetables if absolutely necessary.

---

❖

## ORIENTAL TOSS

*This is delicious when served on a bed of fine egg noodles.*

Serves 6

- [ ] **3 stalks celery, cut into thin strips**
- [ ] **3 carrots, cut into thin strips**
- [ ] **3 zucchini, cut into thin strips**
- [ ] **2 large leeks, cut into thin strips**
- [ ] **1 parsnip, cut into thin strips**
- [ ] **4 oz (125 g) bean sprouts**
- [ ] **2 tablespoons vegetable oil**
- [ ] **1 onion, sliced**
- [ ] **1 tablespoon cornstarch, blended with 2 tablespoons water**
- [ ] **3 tablespoons sesame seeds, toasted**

MARINADE
- [ ] **1 teaspoon grated fresh ginger**
- [ ] **2 cloves garlic, crushed**
- [ ] **¹/₄ cup (60 mL) dry sherry**
- [ ] **¹/₂ cup (125 mL) teriyaki sauce**
- [ ] **4 tablespoons honey, warmed**

1   To make marinade: Combine ginger, garlic, sherry, teriyaki sauce and honey in a large bowl and mix well. Add celery, carrots, zucchini, leeks, parsnip and bean sprouts, and toss to combine. Cover and refrigerate for 1 hour.
2   Heat oil in a wok or skillet and cook onion for 4-5 minutes or until golden. Drain vegetables and reserve half of marinade. Add vegetables to wok and stir-fry for 5 minutes.
3   Combine reserved marinade and cornstarch mixture and stir into vegetables. Bring to the boil, reduce heat and simmer until sauce thickens slightly. Sprinkle with sesame seeds and serve.

---

❖

## FETTUCCINE WITH WINE AND MUSHROOMS

*The perfect way to serve fettuccine – with a magnificent creamy sauce laden with button mushrooms.*

Serves 6

- [ ] **1¹/₄ pounds (600 g) fettuccine**
- [ ] **1 tablespoon olive oil**

MUSHROOM SAUCE
- [ ] **1 tablespoon olive oil**
- [ ] **1 large onion, sliced**
- [ ] **2 cloves garlic, crushed**
- [ ] **16 oz (500 g) button mushrooms, sliced**
- [ ] **1 tablespoon (15 g) butter**
- [ ] **1 tablespoon all-purpose flour**
- [ ] **¹/₄ cup (60 mL) white wine**
- [ ] **1 cup (250 mL) vegetable stock or broth**
- [ ] **¹/₂ cup (125 mL) light cream**
- [ ] **2 tablespoons chopped fresh basil**
- [ ] **freshly ground black pepper**
- [ ] **2 tablespoons grated Parmesan cheese**
- [ ] **2 tablespoons finely snipped fresh chives**

1   Cook fettuccine in boiling water until tender but firm. Drain and toss in oil. Set aside and keep warm.
2   To make sauce: Heat the oil in a saucepan and cook onion and garlic over low heat for 10 minutes or until onion is golden. Stir in the mushrooms and cook for 2 minutes longer. Remove from pan, drain on paper towels and set aside.
3   Melt butter in a clean saucepan, then mix in flour and cook for 2 minutes. Remove from heat and gradually stir in the wine and stock or broth. Cook over medium heat, stirring constantly until sauce boils and thickens. Whisk in cream and stir in mushroom mixture and basil. Season to taste with pepper and cook over low heat until heated through.
4   To serve: Spoon sauce over hot fettuccine and top with Parmesan cheese and chives.

*Spinach Pie, Oriental Toss, Fettuccine with Wine and Mushrooms*

*Win both ways, cooking with nuts, grains, pulses and vegetables: firstly for your wallet, as these dietary staples are remarkably economical; secondly for your health, as there are few foods more nutritious.*

# EASY A TO Z
## *nutrition know-how*

## LEGUMES

**A**dzuki beans. Small reddish-brown beans with a cream-colored seam. Their creamy texture is particularly popular in Japan and China where they are boiled, mashed and sweetened for use in cakes and desserts. They can also be used in soups, pâtés and savory dishes.

**Preparation and cooking:** Cover beans with cold water and soak for 2-2$^1$/2 hours. To cook: Drain, cover with water, then boil gently for 1$^1$/2-2 hours.

*Nutrition: High fiber, low fat. Fair source of protein and iron.*

*3$^1$/2 oz (100 g) raw = 130 Calories (560 kilojoules)*

**B**lack beans. Small, almost round black beans with a white seam. Popular in the West Indies and in Chinese cuisine. They are a sweet-tasting bean that can also be used in soups, salads and savory dishes.

**Preparation and cooking:** Standard preparation. To cook: Drain, cover with water, then boil gently for 30-60 minutes.

*Nutrition: High fiber, low fat. Good source of protein, iron, potassium and thiamine. Fair source of calcium.*

*3$^1$/2 oz (100 g) raw = 340 Calories (1420 kilojoules)*

**B**lack-eyed beans. Small, creamy white, kidney-shaped beans with a black eye also known as black-eyed peas. Brought to Europe and America by slave traders in the 17th century, they are now used widely in soups, baked dishes and pâtés.

**Preparation and cooking:** Standard preparation. To cook: Drain, cover with water, then boil gently for about 1 hour.

*Nutrition: Excellent source of thiamine and fiber. Low in fat. Good source of protein, iron and potassium.*

*3$^1$/2 oz (100 g) raw = 345 Calories (1440 kilojoules)*

**B**orlotti beans. Large, plump, brown, kidney-shaped beans with burgundy markings, also known as Cranberry beans. Popular in Italian cuisine.

**Preparation and cooking:** Standard preparation, or soak. To cook: Drain, cover with water, then boil for 1$^1$/2-2 hours.

*Nutrition: Excellent source of thiamine. High in fiber, low in fat. Good source of protein, iron and potassium. Supplies some calcium.*

*3$^1$/2 oz (100 g) raw = 350 Calories (1460 kilojoules)*

**B**road beans. Flat beans native to North Africa ranging in color from olive green to brown/cream. Initially cultivated by the ancient Egyptians and Greeks. They are known in Europe as Fava beans and are mostly eaten dried. Broad beans are also eaten fresh.

**Preparation and cooking:** Standard preparation. To cook: Drain, cover with water, then boil gently for about 2$^1$/2 hours.

*Nutrition: Low fat. Good source of vitamin C. Fair source of fiber.*

*3$^1$/2 oz (100 g) raw = 70 Calories (300 kilojoules)*

**B** *utter beans.* Native to South America, these large plump, white beans are similar in shape to broad beans. Available fresh, dried, canned and frozen.
**Preparation and cooking:** Standard preparation; if you are going to purée them you will also need to soak the beans. If serving whole, they can just be cooked. To cook: drain, cover with water, then boil gently for about 2 hours.
*Nutrition: Low fat. Good source of protein, iron, dietary fiber, potassium pyridoxine and thiamine. Supplies some calcium.*
*3¹/₂ oz (100 g) raw = 280 Calories (1160 kilojoules)*

**C** *annellini beans.* White kidney beans with square ends. Popular in Italian cuisine. Delicious in soups or salads or in place of haricot beans to make baked beans.
**Preparation and cooking:** Standard preparation. To cook: drain, cover with water, then boil gently for 1¹/₂ hours.
*Nutrition: Low fat. Good source of thiamine, protein, iron and fiber. Fair source of calcium.*
*3¹/₂ oz (100 g) raw = 340 Calories (1420 kilojoules)*

**C** *hickpeas.* Available as white Garbanzo beans or small, brown, Desi Chick peas. Both are round and rough textured with a pointed break at one end. Crunchy and nutty flavor. Popular in Middle Eastern cooking where they are combined with tahini, lemon and garlic to make hummus. In Israel they are used to make a version of

falafal. In Greece, roasted chickpeas are served with drinks.
**Preparation and cooking:** Standard preparation. To cook: drain, cover with water, then boil gently for about 1¹/₂ hours. If you require softened peas, you will also need to soak them.
*Nutrition: High fiber, low fat. Good source of protein, iron and thiamine.*
*3¹/₂ oz (100 g) raw = 360 Calories (1500 kilojoules )*

**H** *aricot/Navy beans.* Small white oval beans. The term haricot derives from medieval times when dried beans were used chiefly in a pot containing a haricot of meat. Probably best known for their use in commercial baked beans, they were commonly served to the U.S. Navy, hence the alternate name. These beans are also delicious in baked dishes.
**Preparation and cooking:** Standard preparation. To cook: drain, cover with water, then boil gently for 1¹/₂ hours.
*Nutrition: High fiber, low fat. Good source of protein, iron, thiamine and potassium. Fair source of calcium and riboflavin.*
*3¹/₂ oz (100 g) raw = 275 Calories (1150 kilojoules)*

**L** *entils.* Popular in European and Indian cuisine, lentils are available in brown, green, orange, yellow and black. They are lens-shaped and may be bought whole or split. Used in soups and baked dishes, they are also the main ingredient of the well-known Indian dip, dahl.

**Preparation and cooking:** No preparation required. To cook: cover with water, then boil. Red lentils will take about 30 minutes and green lentils 1-1¹/₂ hours.
*Nutrition: High fiber, low fat. Good source of protein, iron, potassium pyridoxine, thiamine and riboflavin.*
*3¹/₂ oz (100 g) raw = 330 calories (1370 kilojoules)*

**L** *ima beans.* Native to South America, lima beans are flat kidney-shaped beans which can be either small and green or large and white. They have a soft floury texture and are popular in both salads and hot dishes.
**Preparation and cooking:** Standard preparation. To cook: drain, cover with water, then boil gently for 1-1¹/₂ hours.
*Nutrition: Low fat. Fair source of vitamin C, protein, dietary fiber and iron.*
*3¹/₂ oz (100 g) raw = 115 Calories (475 kilojoules)*

**M** *ung beans.* Widely cultivated in India and China, these small olive green beans are available whole, split and skinless. They are commonly used in stews and salads but are best known in their sprouted form as bean sprouts.
**Preparation and cooking:** No preparation is required. To cook: cover with water and boil gently for 45-60 minutes.
*Nutrition: High fiber, low fat. Good source of protein, iron, thiamine, riboflavin and folate. Some potassium and calcium.*
*3¹/₂ oz (100 g) raw = 235 Calories (980 kilojoules)*

**P**igeon peas. Native to Africa, these small round cream or brown peas are also eaten in India and the Caribbean. They are delicious puréed and added to stews or mixed in salads.
**Preparation and cooking:** Standard preparation. To cook: Drain, cover with water, then cook for 30-60 minutes.
*Nutrition: Good source of dietary fiber, protein, iron and potassium. Some calcium.*
*3¹/₂ oz (100 g) raw = 340 Calories (1430 kilojoules)*

**R**ed kidney beans. Sweet-tasting, red, kidney-shaped beans. Mostly used in soups, stews and salads. Traditionally used in Creole cooking and in the Mexican dish chili con carne.
**Preparation and cooking:** Standard preparation. To cook: Drain, cover with water, boil rapidly for 10 -15 minutes, then cook for 1-1¹/₂ hours.
*Nutrition: High fiber. Good source of protein, iron, potassium, thiamine and pyridoxine. Fair source of calcium.*
*3¹/₂ oz (100 g) raw = 275 Calories (1140 kilojoules)*

**S**oybeans. These small, hard, oval, beige beans are extremely versatile. Originally cultivated in China, soybeans are possibly the most nutritious of all beans and are best known for their by-products which include soy sauce, tofu (bean curd), miso (fermented soybeans), and tempeh (fermented bean paste).

Soybeans are also used to make textured vegetable protein (TVP) and soybean milk.
**Preparation and cooking:** Standard preparation. To cook: Drain, cover with water, then boil gently for 3¹/₂-4 hours.
*Nutrition: Excellent source of thiamine. Good source of dietary fiber, protein, iron and potassium. Some calcium.*
*3¹/₂ oz (100 g) raw = 405 Calories (1694 kilojoules)*

**S**plit peas. Green and yellow peas are available. The green pea is traditionally used in the English pease pudding. The yellow variety is puréed for soup. In Sweden, this soup is traditionally served on a Thursday evening, to commemorate the last supper of the unpopular King Eric XIV who was done in through a dash of arsenic in his split pea soup!
**Preparation and cooking:** No preparation necessary. To cook: Cover with water, then boil gently for 1-1¹/₂ hours, without stirring.
*Nutrition: High fiber, low fat. Good source of thiamine, protein and iron.*
*3¹/₂ oz (100 g) raw = 315 Calories (1320 kilojoules)*

**W**hole dried peas. One of the tastiest variety of peas. They are used in purées or Cornish pasties, pea soup, pease pudding, or as a fresh pea substitute.
**Preparation and cooking:** Soak overnight with a pinch of baking soda. To cook: Drain, cover with water, then boil gently for 1 hour.
*Nutrition: Good source of thiamine, protein, potassium, fiber and iron.*
*3¹/₂ oz (100 g) raw = 285 Calories (1200 kilojoules)*

# NUTS

**A**lmonds. Native to the Eastern Mediterranean regions, almonds are the kernels of the fruit of the almond tree. These nuts feature widely in cooking and are used in both sweet and savory dishes. The nut is encased in a light brown pitted shell and is a long, flat, oval, creamy-colored nut.
*Nutrition: Excellent source of vitamin E. Good source of fiber and riboflavin. Some iron, protein and potassium.*
*3¹/₂ oz (100 g) = 558 Calories (2335 kilojoules)*
*Fats: 68% mono-unsaturated, 22% polyunsaturated, 10% saturated*

**B**razil nuts. A creamy-colored nut with a dark brown skin encased in an angular dull brown grey-colored shell. Brazil nuts can be used in both sweet and savory dishes.
*Nutrition: Good source of vitamin E and thiamine. Useful source of protein, iron and dietary fiber.*
*3¹/₂ oz (100 g) = 608 Calories (2545 kilojoules)*
*Fats: 36% mono-unsaturated, 38% polyunsaturated, 26% saturated*

**C**ashew nuts. Kidney-shaped nuts native to Brazil and the West Indies. These nuts were brought to the rest of the world by Portuguese explorers. Cashews are used widely in sweet and savory dishes. In Brazil they are also used

for making wine and for the production of anacard, the famous cashew nut vinegar.
*Nutrition: Useful source of protein, iron and folic acid. Some dietary fiber.*
*3¹/₂ oz (100 g) = 575 Calories (2400 kilojoules).*
*Fats: 62% mono-saturated, 18% polyunsaturated, 20% saturated*

**Chestnuts.** Large, round, greyish-white nuts with a point at one end, encased in a soft reddish brown shell. Often used in desserts, pâtés and stuffings. In Italy, chestnuts are stewed in wine, while in France braised or puréed nuts provide the traditional garnish for poultry.
*Nutrition: Low in fat. Some B vitamins, potassium and dietary fiber.*
*3¹/₂ oz (100 g) = 245 Calories (1025 kilojoules)*
*Fats: Negligible*

**Coconuts.** The coconut tree is native to Malaya. The white flesh and milk of the coconut is encased in a rough brown husk which is surrounded by a green pod. Supplying a huge amount of products such as milk, butter, cream and oil, coconut is extremely versatile and is used widely in both sweet and savory cooking.
*Nutrition: Good source of fiber, small quantities of other vitamins and minerals.*
*3¹/₂ oz (100 g) fresh = 345 Calories (1445 kilojoules)*
*Fats: 94% saturated, 5% mono-unsaturated, 1% polyunsaturated*

**Hazelnuts.** Small, round, light brown nuts with a pointed end, encased in a hard brown shell. Hazelnuts, also known as filberts, are native to North America, South East Europe and Asia. Hazelnuts can be used in desserts, stuffings and as a spread.
*Nutrition: Rich in vitamin E. Useful amounts of thiamine, pyridoxine and folic acid.*
*3¹/₂ oz (100 g) = 375 Calories (1570 kilojoules)*
*Fats: 82% mono-unsaturated, 10% polyunsaturated, 8% saturated*

**Macadamia nuts.** Native to Australia, these hard, smooth, brownish, spherical nuts have a creamy, bittersweet flavor. Macadamia nuts can be used in both sweet and savory dishes.
*Nutrition: Useful source of thiamine. Small amounts of fiber.*
*3¹/₂ oz (100 g) = 718 Calories (3005 kilojoules)*
*Fats: 82% mono-unsaturated, 2% poly-unsaturated, 16% saturated*

**Peanuts.** Although the most popular of all nuts, peanuts are not a true nut but the pods of a leguminous plant native to South America. Two peanut kernels are encased in each soft brown shell. Peanuts are used predominantly as a cocktail snack, in peanut butter and peanut oil. They are widely

used in savory dishes and are a favorite on top of ice cream.
*Nutrition: Good source of vitamin E, niacin, thiamine and folic acid. Useful source of protein, potassium, pyridoxine and dietary fiber.*
*3¹/₂ oz (100 g) = 565 Calories (2365 kilojoules)*
*Fats: 52% mono-unsaturated, 33% polyunsaturated, 15% saturated*

**Pecans.** Long, flat, ridged oval-shaped nuts encased in a brittle reddish-brown shell. Native to the southern states of America, they were used widely by Indian tribes, hence their Indian name. Popular in the dessert pecan pie, pecans can also be used in savory dishes and stuffings.
*Nutrition: Useful source of thiamine. Some protein and dietary fiber.*
*3¹/₂ oz (100 g) = 660 Calories (2760 kilojoules)*
*Fats: 66% mono-unsaturated, 26% polyunsaturated, 8% saturated*

**Pine nuts.** Small, soft, creamy colored kernels from the cones of a specific pine tree native to Europe, Mexico and southwest America. Pine nuts are classically found in Mediterranean cooking where they are used to make pesto sauce or to stuff vegetables.
*Nutrition: Good source of iron, vitamin E and thiamine. Useful source of protein and dietary fiber.*
*3¹/₂ oz (100 g) = 515 Calories (2155 kilojoules)*
*Fats: 40% mono-unsaturated, 44% polyunsaturated, 16% saturated*

**P**istachio nuts. Exquisite, pale green nuts with half open shells. Native to the Middle East, they are used in both sweet and savory dishes. The best Turkish Delight and nougat contains pistachio nuts.
*Nutrition: Useful source of thiamine, iron and potassium. Small quantities of other vitamins, minerals and dietary fiber.*
*3¹/₂ oz (100 g) = 577 Calories (2415 kilojoules)*
*Fats: 71% mono-unsaturated, 16% polyunsaturated, 13% saturated*

**W**alnuts. Fruit of the walnut tree, these nuts are thought to have originated from ancient Persia or China. A creamy brown shell encases the kernel which is in two distinct halves. Walnuts are used extensively in sweet and savory cooking. Walnut oil makes exquisite salad dressing.
*Nutrition: Useful source of pyridoxine, thiamine and folic acid. Some protein and dietary fiber.*
*3¹/₂ oz (100 g) = 517 Calories (2165 kilojoules)*
*Fats: 24% mono-unsaturated, 67% polyunsaturated, 9% saturated*

# SEEDS

**P**oppy seeds. Very small, round, black seeds with a distinctive warm dusty flavor, native to the northeast Mediterranean region. Although related to the opium poppy, they lack narcotic properties. Generally used on top of breads and crackers or in the traditional poppy seed cake.
*Nutrition: As amounts consumed are usually small, nutritional value is insignificant.*
*3¹/₂ oz (100 g) – 16 Calories (65 kilojoules)*

**P**umpkin seeds. A dull green kernel enclosed in a flat creamy-white shell. Generally eaten as a snack or health food.
*Nutrition: Good source of iron and vitamin E. Provide useful amounts of protein, potassium, thiamine and riboflavin if eaten in large quantities.*
*3¹/₂ oz (100 g) = 540 Calories (2265 kilojoules)*
*Fats: 32% mono-unsaturated, 48% polyunsaturated, 20% saturated*

**S**esame seeds. Small, flat, cream-colored seeds from the sesame plant. Originally from Turkey, these seeds have a nutty taste and are probably the most familiar topping on bread. Sesame seeds are used to make the spread tahini which is a component of hummus. They are also used to make the sweet halva.
*Nutrition: In the quantities usually consumed they provide small amounts of iron and vitamin E.*
*3¹/₂ oz (100 g) = 586 Calories (2460 kilojoules)*
*Fats: 40% mono-unsaturated, 45% polyunsaturated, 15% saturated*

**S**unflower seeds. Medium, flat, oval beige kernels encased in a fawn and black striped shell, native to North America. Generally used as a topping for breads, health food cakes or cookies. Also used to make safflower oil and margarine.
*Nutrition: Good source of iron and vitamin E. Provides useful amounts of protein and niacin. Some thiamine, riboflavin and dietary fiber.*
*3¹/₂ oz (100 g) = 570 Calories (2385 kilojoules)*
*Fats: 20% mono-unsaturated, 69% polyunsaturated, 11% saturated*

# GRAINS

**B**arley. In ancient times, barley was used to make bread. Nowadays, it is more often used as a thickening agent. Barley has a pleasant nutty taste and can be eaten as pot or Scotch barley, pearl barley or barley meal. Preparation and cooking vary according to recipe.
*Nutrition: Low fat, high in fiber, carbohydrate, iron, thiamine and niacin.*

**B**uckwheat. Not actually a wheat but a member of the rhubarb family. Used to make Russian kasha, blini and Japanese noodles called soba. Preparation and cooking depend on the recipe.
*Nutrition: Low fat, high in fiber, carbohydrate, thiamine, niacin and riboflavin.*

**C**orn. Once the generic term for all grains, corn is a versatile grain that yields many useful products. Preparation and cooking vary according to recipe.

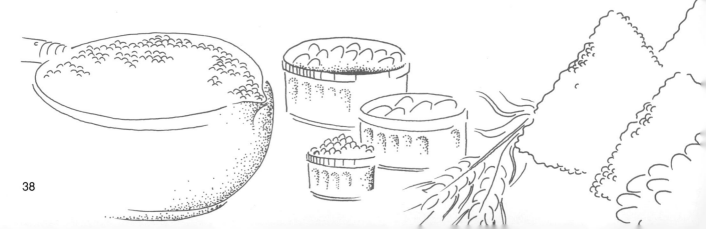

**Corn meal:** Corn meal is used in johnnycakes, hush puppies, and cornbread in the United States. In Italy, it is used to make a type of porridge called polenta. Corn meal is also used to make tortillas.

**Cornflour/cornstarch:** The white heart of the corn kernel ground into a powder. It is generally used as a thickening agent for soups, stews, and sauces.

*Nutrition: Low fat, high in fiber, carbohydrate, protein, iron, niacin and thiamine.*

**Millet and Sorghum.** Closely related to each other, their greatest characteristic is that they swell enormously. Both have a pleasant nutty taste and are best cooked and eaten like rice. In India, millet is combined with black beans to make pancakes called ragi doas. Preparation and cooking depend on the recipe.

*Nutrition: Low in fat, high in carbohydrate, niacin and thiamine. Some iron.*

**Oats.** Among the most nutritious of all cereals, oats are best known for their use in the Scottish breakfast cereal porridge or oatmeal. Oatmeal comes in three grades of varying coarseness. Medium grade is traditionally used to make porridge, while fine grade is used for baking oatcakes, cookies and scones. Preparation and cooking depend on the recipe.

*Nutrition: High in fiber, carbohydrate, thiamine, folate and vitamin E.*

**Rice.** At least one-third of mankind eats rice as a staple food. There are many varieties and no preparation is required. Cooking varies according to the variety of rice and recipe.

**Short-grain rice:** The most popular all-purpose rice, particularly suited to dishes where grains need to cling together.

**Long-grain rice:** Known for its fluffy texture, long-grain rice is good for pilafs, salads and stuffings.

**Brown rice:** The natural unpolished rice that has a distinctive nutty taste.

**Basmati rice:** Grown in Bangladesh and Pakistan, this rice is a delicious, aromatic rice ideal for highly spiced Indian dishes.

**Piedmontese or Arborio rice:** Italian rices that are ideal for absorbing a great deal of liquid. Generally used for risotto, paella or jambalaya.

**Wild rice:** Although related to the rice family, wild rice is actually a seed from an aquatic grass which grows in North America. It has an appealing distinctive nutty flavor. It is quite expensive, and is used more commonly in gourmet cooking.

**Ground rice and rice flour:** Mostly used for desserts and cakes, or as a thickener.

*Nutrition: Low fat, high in fiber, carbohydrate, thiamine, niacin and folate.*

**Rye.** A strong-flavored grain commonly used in Scandinavia, Russia and Germany. Rye is used to make pumpernickel and black breads, as well as many crispbreads. It is also the basis of the alcoholic drinks, whiskey, gin and beer. Preparation and cooking depend on the recipe.

*Nutrition: Low fat, high in fiber, thiamine, riboflavin, pyridoxine and folate.*

**Wheat.** Wheat is available in various forms. Preparation and cooking vary according to variety and recipe.

**Wholewheat grain:** Can be eaten in the same way as rice or as a type of porridge called "frumenty".

**Cracked or kibbled wheat:** Wholewheat grain which has been cracked between rollers and is eaten in the same way as the wholewheat grain.

**Burghul or bulgur:** Cracked wheat that has been hulled and parboiled, giving the wheat a lighter texture and making it easier to cook. Used in the Lebanese salad tabbouleh.

**Bran:** The papery thin layer of the wheat grain. Bran is an excellent source of dietary fiber.

**Wheat germ:** The heart of the wheat grain. Wheat germ may be extracted from the wheat grain to improve its keeping qualities. Wheat germ is often eaten as a topping on cereal.

**Semolina:** Semolina is the floury part of the wheat grain which is left over when the bran and wheat germ are removed. Semolina is used for breakfast cereal or desserts. Flour-coated semolina is used to make couscous, a traditional North African dish.

**Plain wholewheat flour:** Wholewheat flour is the flour made from the wholewheat grain.

*Nutrition: Low fat, high in fiber and carbohydrate. Good source of B vitamins and iron.*

*Changing your eating habits requires commitment – easy once you taste our delicious vegetarian recipes! Don't launch headlong into vegetarianism, or any major change of eating habits, without thinking about your nutritional needs.*

# VEGETARIAN
## essentials

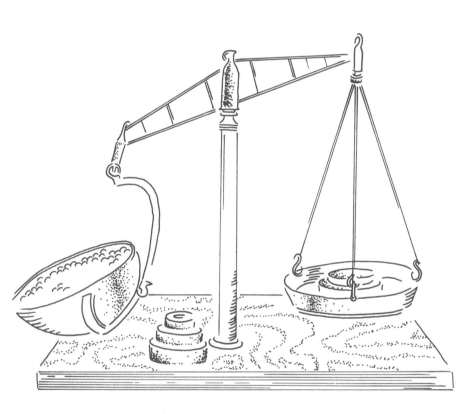

*Changing to a vegetarian diet*
✧ Use the following tips as a guideline if you are changing to a vegetarian diet.
✧ Change to a vegetarian diet gradually.
✧ Start by having one vegetarian meal each week and build up slowly.
✧ Don't commence a strict vegetarian diet overnight. The body and palate need time to adapt!
✧ Do some reading on nutrition. If you are unsure about anything, you should consult a dietitian.
✧ Do not change your diet radically when pregnant or breastfeeding. Small, gradual change is best. Get some professional advice.
✧ Small children have high nutrition requirements. Diets containing milk products should be followed.

*Types of vegetarians*
Vegetarians are generally classified according to the degree to which animal products are consumed or avoided.
✧ Total vegetarians, vegans, consume no animal products.
✧ Lacto-ovo vegetarians eat no animal flesh, but include milk products and eggs in their diet.
✧ Lacto vegetarians consume milk products but no eggs.
✧ Semi- or partial vegetarians consume some groups of animal foods but not all; red meat is excluded but white meats such as poultry or fish may be eaten.
✧ Alternative or "new" vegetarians – who include fruitarians (fruit only) and followers of the Zen macrobiotic diet – are technically vegetarian. Strict versions of these diets fail to provide adequate nutrients to sustain good health. In general, stricter diets have a greater potential for nutritional inadequacy.

| WATCH POINTS FOR VEGETARIANS | | |
| --- | --- | --- |
| DIET | FOODS AVOIDED | NUTRIENTS AT RISK |
| Partial Vegetarians | Meat and/or poultry, fish | Iron |
| Lacto-Ovo Vegetarians | Meat, poultry, fish | Iron, zinc |
| Lacto Vegetarians | Meat, poultry, fish, eggs | Energy, iron, zinc |
| Vegan Vegetarians | Meat, poultry, fish, eggs, dairy foods | Energy, protein, iron, calcium, zinc, vitamin B12 |
| Alternative Vegetarians | Generally as vegan, or more restrictive | As above plus others, depending on level of restriction |

## Protein

✦ Adults require protein on a daily basis to repair and replace existing proteins.

✦ During certain stages of life – childhood, adolescence and pregnancy – more protein is required as new body tissues are being built.

✦ Protein requirements are increased during breastfeeding, as protein is lost in the mother's milk.

✦ Proteins are made up of smaller units called amino acids – these are the building blocks of protein.

✦ To make protein, the body requires the twenty-two amino acids in the appropriate quantities and proportions.

✦ The body can manufacture all but eight of the amino acids (nine in infants). These are known as the essential amino acids, as they should be an essential part of the diet.

✦ Inadequate consumption of essential amino acids slows down the manufacture of new proteins and will result in weight loss and delayed growth.

✦ Dietary proteins are found in animal products such as meat, poultry, seafood, eggs and dairy products. Plant foods such as legumes, nuts, seeds and cereals also supply protein.

✦ Animal products such as meat, poultry, seafood, eggs, milk, cheese and yogurt contain more protein than plant foods. These animal proteins are known as complete proteins since they contain the eight essential amino acids in sufficient quantity and proportion to supply the body with what it needs.

✦ Proteins found in plant foods like grains, nuts, legumes, and seeds are present in smaller amounts and are known as incomplete proteins as they lack at least one of the essential amino acids.

✦ Eating a combination of incomplete proteins each day, preferably at the same meal, ensures that all the essential amino acids are supplied in the diet to provide your body with what it needs.

✦ This combining of foods is known as protein complementation.

# THE COMPLETE PROTEIN STORY

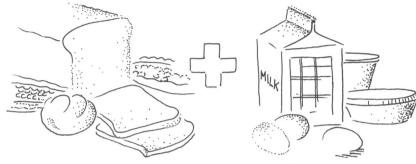

**Grains**
bread, rice, pasta
barley, rye, oats

**Milk Products**
milk, cheese, yogurt

Rolled oats with milk
Pasta or rice with cheese
Rice custard
Cheese on bread or toast
Yogurt with pasta or rice

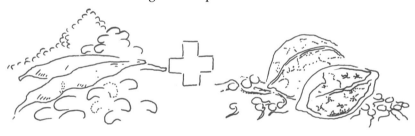

**Legumes**
dried peas, beans,
lentils, nuts

**Seeds**
sesame, sunflower seeds

Nut and seed mixed snack
Hummus
Stir-fry beans and seeds

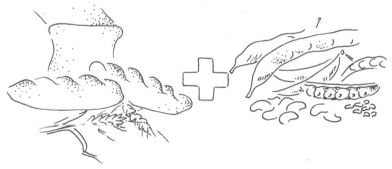

**Grains**
bread, rice, pasta
barley, rye oats

**Legumes**
dried peas, beans, lentils

Corn tortillas and beans
Rice with dried beans, lentils or nuts
Tofu or dahl with rice
Peanut butter or baked beans on bread or toast

# THE VEGETARIAN FAMILY

## Vegetarian mothers

✧ Pregnancy and breastfeeding will increase the need for a number of nutrients (energy, protein, calcium, iron, zinc, vitamins A, C, and many of the B vitamins).

✧ Well-balanced vegetarian diets will meet these increased needs.

✧ Achieving adequate weight gain during pregnancy is sometimes difficult for vegetarian women, particularly anyone who was a little underweight before pregnancy.

✧ Increased food intake between meals generally helps, as does an increased intake of dairy foods or soy milk substitutes (these should be calcium and B12 fortified).

✧ Physicians frequently prescribe iron and folate (a form of vitamin B) supplements for pregnant vegetarian women as a precautionary measure.

✧ Use of supplements during pregnancy or breastfeeding is best coordinated by a physician or dietitian.

✧ Excessive use of supplements is not recommended.

✧ Supplements of vitamin B12 are only necessary for some vegan vegetarians.

✧ Well-nourished women who eat a vegetarian diet can breastfeed just as successfully as non-vegetarians.

✧ Since the energy demands of breastfeeding are quite substantial, some women have problems with weight loss.

✧ Adequate energy, protein, calcium, iron and vitamin B12 intake is essential for mothers at this time.

✧ A well-balanced diet which contains milk or a fortified soy drink will optimize nutrient intake.

## Vegetarian children

✧ Infants and children who consume a well-planned vegetarian diet which includes dairy products can meet their nutritional requirements and maintain normal growth.

✧ As the vegetarian diet is high in fiber, and therefore of a bulky nature, it is difficult for children to get enough energy and protein – they simply cannot eat enough food! If this occurs, their growth may be delayed.

✧ The vegan diet is generally not recommended for infants and children unless it is supplemented to meet their nutritional needs.

✧ Inadequate intakes of energy, protein, calcium, iron, riboflavin and vitamin B12 have been reported in children on strict vegan diets. This is most probably because of their inability to eat enough.

✧ The risks of inadequate nutrient intake seem to be highest after weaning, as this is the most rapid stage of growth.

## Vegetarian teenagers

✧ Inadequate nutrient intakes (energy, protein, calcium, iron, zinc and vitamin A) have also been reported in vegetarian teenagers.

✧ The growth spurt in teenage years increases nutritional needs. The risks are again higher for those who follow vegan diets.

✧ Teenagers live busy lives and it is often difficult for parents to control what teenagers are eating. One way to ensure at least one good meal a day is to make sure that your teenager eats a good healthy breakfast.

✧ Keeping healthy and interesting snacks in the pantry or refrigerator will also help ensure that your teenager gets enough to eat.

# GETTING THE BALANCE RIGHT

*The following guide will help you get to know your sources of protein, vitamins and minerals.*

| | |
|---|---|
| *Protein* | Eggs, milk, cheese, yogurt, soy milk, tofu, vegetarian meat analogs (such as nut meat, textured vegetable protein), legumes (such as dried peas, beans and lentils), nuts, bread, rice, pasta, barley and other grains are the major sources of protein in a vegetarian diet. |
| *Vitamin B12* | Eggs, milk, cheese, yogurt, fortified soy products (such as fortified soy milk) are the main sources of vitamin B12 in a vegetarian diet. Since bacteria can make vitamin B12 through a fermentation process, fermented foods (perhaps even the fermentation of ingested foods which occurs in the mouth and intestine) are an additional, but less reliable source of vitamin B12 in a vegetarian diet. |
| *Vitamin D* | Found in eggs, margarine, butter, cream, milk and milk products, vitamin D can also be made by the body when it is exposed to sunlight. |
| *Riboflavin* | Dairy foods (milk, cheese and yogurt), eggs, legumes (dried peas, beans, and lentils), green leafy vegetables (broccoli and spinach), almonds, yeast extracts and fortified breakfast cereals are important sources of riboflavin in any diet. |
| *Calcium* | Include milk, cheese, yogurt, calcium-enriched soy products (such as tofu, TVP [textured vegetable protein], soy milks – with these products it is important to read the labels), legumes, dark green leafy vegetables (broccoli, kale), almonds, sesame seeds, tahini (sesame seed paste) in your diet to ensure adequate calcium intake. |
| *Iron* | Legumes, green leafy vegetables, breads, grains and cereals – especially fortified breakfast cereals – are the major sources of iron in a vegetarian diet. |
| *Zinc* | Wholegrain cereals, rice, legumes (dried peas, beans and lentils) and nuts are the important sources of zinc in a vegetarian diet. |

# 7 GOOD REASONS TO EAT VEGETARIAN

**Less obesity**

Studies of vegetarians report that they are more likely to have a desirable body weight when compared with non-vegetarians, possibly due to the high complex carbohydrate/fiber, low-fat nature of their diet.

**Less diabetes**

Late or maturity onset diabetes, which, as the name suggests, mostly occurs in middle or older age groups, is associated with obesity. The lower incidence of obesity in vegetarians reduces their risk of developing diabetes. The vegetarian diet, being high in complex carbohydrate and fiber whilst low in fat, is ideal for both the prevention and management of diabetes.

**Less blood pressure**

Elevated blood pressure, also known as hypertension, is related to obesity, and in some individuals, to a high salt intake. Since vegetarians tend to be leaner than non-vegetarians, as a group they have a reduced risk of developing high blood pressure. Many vegetarian diets are also reduced in salt intake.

**Less heart disease**

Vegetarians are found to have a reduced incidence of heart disease. This is not surprising since they have a lower incidence of obesity, high blood pressure, diabetes, high cholesterol and smoking. The low saturated fat and high fiber diet is also considered to be a major benefit.

**Less cancer**

Death from all types of cancer is lower in vegetarians than in non-vegetarians. The virtual absence of smoking and the high fiber intake of vegetarians is considered to reduce the risk of developing lung and bowel cancer respectively. Large intakes of dark green or yellow vegetables, which supply carotene, are thought to generally protect the body against developing cancer (carotene is converted to vitamin A in the body). Less obesity and a lower fat intake has been proposed as an explanation for the lower incidence of breast cancer in vegetarian women.

**Less bowel disease**

Constipation, hemorrhoids and diverticular disease are less common in vegetarians. The high fiber content of their diet improves bowel regularity, which subsequently reduces their risk of developing these diseases.

**Longevity**

The vegetarians' diet lowers their risk of premature death from heart disease, diabetes and cancers, and enhances their quality of life by reducing illnesses associated with these chronic diseases.

 # 7 WATCHPOINTS FOR VEGETARIANS

**Inadequate protein**

Although the amount and quality of protein is less in vegetables and grains than in flesh foods, the appropriate combination of plant foods will meet the body's protein needs.

**Vitamin B12**

Nutritional deficiencies rarely occur in adults as the body stores approximately 1000 times its daily requirement. This store can last for up to five years. In practical terms, deficiency is more often found in infants and children of vegan parents. The pregnant/breastfeeding vegan mother must therefore take care to ensure that her vitamin B12 intake is adequate.

**Vitamin D**

The body can also manufacture vitamin D, providing that the skin is exposed to some sunlight. Cod liver oil is the richest dietary source of vitamin D and was often used to treat rickets, the disease associated with a deficiency of vitamin D. This deficiency is rare and essentially only occurs in those persons who get no exposure to sunlight.

**Fat**

While vegetarian diets are generally low in fat, diets which contain excessive amounts of fat, oils and full-cream dairy foods can be high in fat. To reduce fat, choose reduced-fat dairy foods and minimize intake of fats and oils.

**Calcium**

Dairy foods are the main source of calcium in the Western diet, although dark green leafy vegetables, legumes, nuts and seeds are useful sources of calcium. Vegetarians who include dairy products in their diets satisfy their calcium requirements most readily. Calcium-fortified products are recommended for vegans.

**Iron**

An adequate iron intake is necessary to prevent iron-deficiency anemia, the symptoms of which include fatigue, shortness of breath and, in severe cases, palpitations. Although iron is found in vegetables, legumes, and cereals, there is generally less than in flesh foods. Iron in plant foods is also less well absorbed. Vitamin C, found in citrus fruits and juices, aids the absorption of iron from plant foods.

**Zinc**

Although zinc is found in a large variety of plant foods, its availability to the body is questionable. Phytic acid, found in grains, is considered to reduce the absorption of zinc, although the process of bread-making lowers phytates and improves zinc availability from bread and bread products. Zinc is essential for protein and carbohydrate metabolism. Most vegetarian diets are adequate in zinc.

*You can't beat the crunch of home-grown sprouts.*
*Many people today are lavish in their praise of both raw*
*foods and living foods. Sprouts are considered*
*to be the perfect combination.*

# SPROUTING
## *know-how*

---

*How to sprout*

1   Place one cup of seeds in a wide-mouthed large glass jar and cover with water at room temperature.

2   Cover opening with a piece of loosely woven cloth or a double thickness of cheesecloth and secure with a strong rubber band. Allow seeds to soak overnight; this encourages germination.

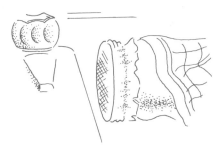

3   The next day, drain off the water. Rinse the seeds with fresh water and drain again. Lay the jar on its side to allow for circulation of air around the seeds. Place jar in a dark, warm position or cover with a tea-towel.

4   Rinse the seeds thoroughly and drain twice a day until the sprouts form. They must not be allowed to sit in water otherwise they will rot, nor should they ever dry out.

*Seeds sprouts*

✧ Sprouts are the young shoots of various rapidly germinating seed plants. They are an important source of vitamins, rich in proteins and minerals, but low in calories (kilojoules) They are also delicious and easily digestible making them one of the best fast foods around.

✧ Sprouts are so versatile in the kitchen that they can be used daily. They can be tossed raw in salads; stir-fried at the last moment in Chinese-style dishes; added to omelet and scrambled eggs; sprinkled on soups and baked dishes just before serving; used as a tasty garnish; and they make a wonderful sandwich filler.

✧ Seed sprouting is easy, quick and inexpensive. They require very little space and are perfect for the apartment dweller without a garden. They can be grown at any time of the year.

✧ Packages of seeds and kits are available from many health food shops. Kits with a built-in drainage facility are the easiest to use. However, a large glass jar and a piece of loosely woven cloth (found at home) are just as efficient.

✧ As seeds increase in volume up to ten times, it is important to choose a glass jar big enough to allow for this.

✧ Always buy seeds that are specifically labeled for sprouting as these will be untreated with chemicals.

✧ Store the sprouts in a plastic bag in the refrigerator to prevent drying. They are best eaten as soon as possible, but will remain in good condition for a few days.

✧ Mustard and cress will grow taller than jar-sprouted seeds if, after an overnight soaking, they are placed on a base of wet cotton balls spread across a plate. Water twice a day and harvest with scissors.

✧ Depending on the type of seed and weather, sprouts will be ready within a few days.

✧ Different seeds need different lengths of time to sprout. The best time to eat sprouts is as soon as the first set of tiny green leaves appear.

✧ Some grain seeds can be sprouted in a little soil in shallow seeding trays.

*A dinner party is always fun. This one, with your time planned and exciting dishes to prepare, is sure to please the most discerning diner.*

# THE BUSY
## *entertainer*

---

## THE MENU

Spicy Peanut Soup

❖

Brown Rice and Vegetable Pie
Two-Pea Salad
Curried Beet and Apple Salad
Squash and Parsnip Fries

❖

Hazelnut Ripple Ice Cream

❖

Herbal Tea
Coconut and Walnut Barfi

---

❖

## SPICY PEANUT SOUP

*Fragrant with Indian spices – a quickly prepared soup that has an exotic flavor.*

Serves 6

- ☐ **3 tablespoons (45 g) margarine**
- ☐ **1 onion, finely chopped**
- ☐ **1 clove garlic, crushed**
- ☐ **1 teaspoon curry powder**
- ☐ **3 cups (750 mL) vegetable stock or broth**
- ☐ **3 cups (750 mL) milk**
- ☐ **1 tablespoon cornstarch, blended with 4 tablespoons milk**
- ☐ **1¹/₂ pounds (750 g) roasted peanuts, ground**
- ☐ **¹/₂ cup (125 g) dairy sour cream**

1   Melt margarine in a large saucepan and cook onion, garlic and curry powder for 4-5 minutes, or until onion softens. Add stock, milk and cornstarch mixture.
2   Bring to the boil, stirring occasionally. Reduce heat and simmer for 15-20 minutes. Stir in peanuts. To serve: Swirl a spoonful of sour cream through each bowl of soup.

❖

## SQUASH AND PARSNIP FRIES

Serves 6

- ☐ **olive oil for deep frying**
- ☐ **1¹/₂ pounds (750 g) butternut squash, peeled, seeded and cut into thick strips**
- ☐ **1¹/₂ pounds (750 g) parsnip, peeled and cut into thick strips**
- ☐ **1 tablespoon ground cumin**
- ☐ **¹/₂ cup (60 g) grated Parmesan cheese**

1   Heat oil in a deep saucepan. Cook squash and parsnip for 6 minutes. Drain on paper towels and set aside.
2   Just prior to serving, reheat the oil and cook fries for 3-4 minutes or until golden brown and crisp. Drain on paper towels.
3   Combine cumin and Parmesan cheese and toss fries in mixture to coat well.

❖

## TWO-PEA SALAD

Serves 6

- ☐ **16 oz (500 g) frozen peas**
- ☐ **5 oz (155 g) snow peas, trimmed**
- ☐ **1 clove garlic, crushed**
- ☐ **2 tablespoons vegetable oil**
- ☐ **2 teaspoons lemon juice**
- ☐ **1 small onion, thinly sliced**

1   Drop frozen peas into a saucepan of boiling water and cook for 3-4 minutes. Add snow peas for the last minute of cooking. Drain and refresh under cold running water.
2   Spoon peas into a salad bowl and season to taste. Combine garlic, oil and lemon juice. Toss through salad and fold through onion.

## THE FINAL TOUCH

An attractively folded napkin adds the final touch to a pretty table. This fold known as the fan is popular and easy to do. It works best with a well-starched or heavy paper napkin.

1   Fold the napkin in half lengthways, then starting at one of the short ends fold the napkin backwards and forwards in concertina style folds to halfway along the length.

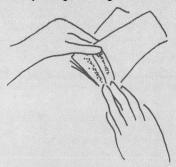

2   Hold the folds firmly and fold the napkin lengthways down the middle to bring both ends of the concertina together. Keep the folds in position with one hand and fold the unfolded flap of the napkin over and across the diagonal.

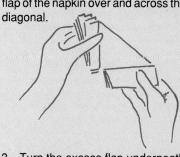

3   Turn the excess flap underneath to support and balance the napkin. Let go of the pleats and allow the fan to fall into position.

## BROWN RICE AND VEGETABLE PIE

Serves 6

- ☐ **10 oz (315 g) cooked brown rice**
- ☐ **8 oz (250 g) shredded Cheddar cheese**
- ☐ **4 tablespoons grated Parmesan cheese**
- ☐ **2 green onions, chopped**
- ☐ **2 zucchini, shredded**
- ☐ **1 carrot, peeled and shredded**
- ☐ **5 oz (155 g) canned asparagus cuts, drained**
- ☐ **3 tablespoons pine nuts, toasted**
- ☐ **3 eggs, lightly beaten**
- ☐ **3/4 cup (200 g) plain low-fat yogurt**
- ☐ **freshly ground black pepper**

1   Combine rice, Cheddar and Parmesan cheeses, green onions, zucchini, carrot, asparagus, pine nuts, eggs and yogurt. Season to taste with pepper.

2   Spoon mixture into a deep well-greased springform pan. Bake at 400°F (200°C) for 40 minutes or until firm. Cut into wedges to serve.

❖

## CURRIED BEET AND APPLE SALAD

Serves 6

- ☐ **1 bunch watercress**
- ☐ **2 green apples, cored and cut into thin slices**
- ☐ **1 tablespoon lemon juice**
- ☐ **2 large beets, cooked, peeled and cut into wedges**
- ☐ **2 green onions, chopped**
- ☐ **2 oz (60 g) pecans**

CURRY DRESSING
- ☐ **2 cloves garlic, crushed**
- ☐ **1 teaspoon grated fresh ginger**
- ☐ **1/2 teaspoon ground cumin**
- ☐ **1/2 teaspoon ground coriander**
- ☐ **1/4 teaspoon chili powder**
- ☐ **2 tablespoons lemon juice**
- ☐ **4 tablespoons vegetable oil**
- ☐ **freshly ground black pepper**

1   To make dressing: Mix garlic, ginger, cumin, coriander and chili powder to make a paste. Whisk in lemon juice and oil and season to taste with pepper. Place watercress in a serving bowl and pour over half the dressing. Toss to combine.

2   Toss apples in lemon juice. Top watercress with beets then apples, green onions and pecans, and pour over remaining dressing.

## HAZELNUT RIPPLE ICE CREAM

*An ice cream with a wonderful texture that will have you coming back again and again for just one more scoop. Serve it with fresh fruits and grated chocolate.*

Serves 6

- ☐ **1/2 cup (125 g) wholewheat bread crumbs made from stale bread**
- ☐ **3/4 cup (125 g) packed brown sugar**
- ☐ **2 oz (60 g) roasted hazelnuts, finely chopped**
- ☐ **11/2 teaspoons ground cinnamon**
- ☐ **1 teaspoon ground mixed spice**
- ☐ **4 cups (1 litre) vanilla ice cream, softened slightly**

1   Combine bread crumbs, sugar and hazelnuts. Place on a cookie sheet and roast at 400°F (200°C) for 12-15 minutes, tossing with a spoon occasionally, or until golden and crunchy.

2   Combine bread crumb mixture, cinnamon and mixed spice. Fold into ice cream. Pour into an aluminum foil-lined freezer tray and freeze until firm.

---

### HERBAL TEAS

Herbal teas are available from all health food shops and some super-markets. There are many varieties to choose from, and they are a soothing alternative to coffee.

---

❖

## COCONUT AND WALNUT BARFI

Makes 25

- ☐ **2 tablespoons (30 g) ghee (clarified butter)**
- ☐ **1 cup (250 mL) canned coconut milk**
- ☐ **10 oz (315 g) grated or shredded coconut**
- ☐ **21/4 cups (250 g) full cream milk powder**
- ☐ **1/2 cup (125 g) superfine sugar**
- ☐ **1 teaspoon ground cardamom**
- ☐ **2/3 cup (60 g) walnuts, chopped**
- ☐ **1/3 cup (60 g) dried dates, chopped**

1   Melt ghee in a small saucepan. Add coconut milk, coconut, milk powder, sugar, cardamom, walnuts and dates and mix well. Cook, stirring, over a medium heat for 2 minutes.

2   Spoon mixture into lightly greased

---

9-inch (23 cm) square cake pan. Smooth the surface, cover and refrigerate overnight. To serve: Remove barfi from pan and cut into squares.

*Clockwise from left: Curried Beet and Apple Salad, Hazelnut Ripple Ice Cream, Coconut and Walnut Barfi, Spicy Peanut Soup, Brown Rice and Vegetable Pie wth Two-Pea Salad and Squash and Parsnip Fries*

Plates Limoges Glassware Incorporated Agencies

*There's something special about putting a concoction into the oven and having it fill the air with delicious scents – while simultaneously filling the room with ravenous admirers.*

# A BAKER'S
## *dozen to delight in*

❖

### WHOLEWHEAT CHERRY AND ALMOND BREAD

*An eye-catching, tasty bread that can be served while still warm. Great to serve with coffee in place of dessert.*

Makes 30 slices

- ☐ **2 eggs**
- ☐ **$^1/_2$ cup (125 g) superfine sugar**
- ☐ **1 cup (155 g) whole blanched almonds**
- ☐ **$^2/_3$ cup (125 g) whole red candied cherries**
- ☐ **1 cup (125 g) all-purpose flour, sifted**
- ☐ **1 cup (125 g) wholewheat flour, sifted**
- ☐ **2 teaspoons baking powder**

1   Place eggs and sugar in a bowl and beat with an electric mixer for 6 minutes or until mixture is thick and creamy. Stir in almonds, cherries, all-purpose and wholewheat flours and baking powder.

2   Spread mixture into a greased and lined 3 x 10$^1/_2$-inch (7 x 23 cm) bar pan. Bake at 350°F (180°C) for 40-45 minutes or until firm and browned. Cool bread in pan for 15 minutes before turning onto a wire rack to cool completely. Wrap in aluminum foil and leave overnight.

3   Cut bread into $^1/_8$-inch (3 mm) slices using a sharp knife. Place slices on cookie sheets in single layers and bake at 350°F (180°C) for 10 minutes or until bread is lightly browned and crisp.

---

**COOK'S TIP**

If you have an electric knife, it is ideal for cutting this loaf.

---

❖

### ORANGE AND LIME YOGURT SYRUP CAKE

Serves 10

- ☐ **$^1/_2$ cup (1 stick/125 g) butter**
- ☐ **1 teaspoon grated lime rind**
- ☐ **3 teaspoons grated orange rind**
- ☐ **1 cup (220 g) superfine sugar**
- ☐ **3 eggs**
- ☐ **1$^1/_2$ cups (200 g) all-purpose flour, sifted**
- ☐ **3 teaspoons baking powder**
- ☐ **$^1/_2$ cup (125 g) plain low-fat yogurt**

SYRUP
- ☐ **2 tablespoons lime juice**
- ☐ **3 tablespoons orange juice**
- ☐ **3 tablespoons sugar**

1   Place butter, lime and orange rinds in a large mixing bowl and beat until light and creamy. Add sugar a little at a time, beating well after each addition.

2   Beat in eggs one at a time and mix well. Fold in flour sifted with baking powder alternately with yogurt. Spoon mixture into a greased 8-inch (20 cm) ring cake pan. Bake at 350°F (180°C) for 30-35 minutes or until cooked. Stand in cake pan for 5 minutes, then turn out on a wire rack with a tray underneath.

3   To make syrup: Place lime juice, orange juice and sugar in a saucepan. Cook over medium heat, stirring constantly, until sugar dissolves. Bring mixture to the boil without stirring, and boil for 3 minutes. Remove from heat and pour hot syrup over hot cake. Set aside to cool.

*Wholewheat Cherry and Almond Bread, Strawberry Tarts, Orange and Lime Yogurt Syrup Cake*

Plates J.D. Milner Glass Incorporated Agencies

## QUEEN OF HEARTS

You might like to change the filling and/or topping for the Strawberry Tarts.

**Lemon Tarts:** Replace strawberry jam with lemon butter. Top with topping and cook as for Strawberry Tarts.

**Orange Tarts:** Remove rind and pith from 2 oranges and chop orange flesh. Use in place of strawberry jam. Top with topping and cook as for Strawberry Tarts.

**Marmalade Tarts:** Replace strawberry jam with marmalade. Top with an oat streusel topping. To make oat streusel topping: Place $2/3$ cup (60 g) rolled oats, $1/3$ cup (60 g) packed brown sugar, $1/2$ cup (60 g) wholewheat flour and $1/2$ teaspoon baking powder in a bowl and stir in 3 oz (90 g) margarine, melted. Sprinkle over tarts and cook as for Strawberry Tarts.

**Jam Tarts:** To make plain jam tarts: Fill the tarts with a jam of your choice and omit topping. Cook as for Strawberry Tarts.

❖

## STRAWBERRY TARTS

Makes 24

- ☐ $1/2$ **cup (1 stick/125 g) margarine**
- ☐ $1/4$ **cup (60 g) sugar**
- ☐ **1 egg**
- ☐ **2 teaspoons milk**
- ☐ **2 cups (250 g) all-pupose flour, sifted**
- ☐ **1 teaspoon baking powder**
- ☐ $3/4$ **cup (185 g) strawberry jam**

TOPPING
- ☐ **2 oz (60 g) sugar**
- ☐ **2 oz (60 g) grated or shredded coconut**
- ☐ **1 egg**

1   Place margarine and sugar in a bowl and beat until light and fluffy. Mix in egg and milk, then flour sifted with baking powder. Mix to form a dough. Turn out onto a lightly floured surface and roll out thinly. Cut into rounds using a 3-inch (7.5 cm) cutter and place in lightly greased small muffin pans. Top with a spoonful of jam.

2   To make topping: Place sugar, coconut and egg in a bowl and mix well. Place a spoonful of topping on each tart and bake at 400°F (200°C) for 10-15 minutes, or until tops are golden and bases are cooked.

## CRUNCHY ALMOND HONEY BARS

Makes 30

- ☐ 1 tablespoon (15 g) butter
- ☐ ¹/₂ cup (185 g) honey
- ☐ ¹/₂ cup (60 g) slivered almonds, toasted
- ☐ 4 tablespoons sunflower seeds
- ☐ 2 tablespoons sesame seeds
- ☐ ²/₃ cup (60 g) dry grated coconut
- ☐ 1 oz (30 g) crisp rice cereal

LEMON ICING
- ☐ 1¹/₂ cups (250 g) IOX (confectioners') sugar, sifted
- ☐ 1 tablespoon (15 g) butter
- ☐ 2 tablespoons lemon juice
- ☐ 1 tablespoon water

1 Combine butter and honey in a saucepan and bring to the boil, stirring gently. Add almonds, sunflower and sesame seeds and boil gently, without stirring, for 3 minutes.

2 Remove from heat. Stir in coconut and cereal. Spread into an aluminum foil-lined 8-inch (20 cm) square cake pan and press down firmly. Refrigerate until set.

3 To make icing: Place confectioners' sugar, butter, lemon juice and water in a mixing bowl and beat until smooth.

4 Remove layer from the pan and spread with icing. Cut into thin bars.

*From left: Crunchy Almond Honey Bars, Honey Banana Cake, Chocolate Caramel Bars, Chocolate Potato Cake*

## CHOCOLATE CARAMEL BARS

Makes 25

SHORTBREAD CRUST
- ☐ ¹/₃ cup (100 g) polyunsaturated margarine
- ☐ 3 tablespoons sugar
- ☐ ¹/₂ cup (60 g) cornstarch, sifted
- ☐ ³/₄ cup (100 g) all-purpose flour, sifted

CARAMEL FILLING
- ☐ ¹/₂ cup (1 stick/125 g) margarine
- ☐ ¹/₂ cup (90 g) packed brown sugar
- ☐ 2 tablespoons honey
- ☐ 12¹/₂ oz (400 g) canned sweetened condensed milk
- ☐ 1 teaspoon vanilla extract

TOPPING
- ☐ 6¹/₂ oz (200 g) semisweet (dark) cooking chocolate, melted

1 To make crust: Place margarine and sugar in a bowl and beat until light and fluffy. Mix in cornstarch and flour, turn out onto a lightly floured surface and knead lightly, then press into a greased and lined 7 x 11-inch (18 x 28 cm) shallow cake pan. Bake at 350°F (180°C) for 25 minutes or until firm.

2 To make filling: Place margarine, sugar and honey in a saucepan and heat, stirring until sugar dissolves. Bring to the boil and simmer for 7 minutes, then add condensed milk and vanilla and beat well. Pour over base and bake at 350°F (180°C) for 20 minutes. Allow to cool completely.

3 Spread topping over filling and chill until set. Store in a cool place. Cut into squares to serve.

## CHOCOLATE POTATO CAKE

Serves 10

- ☐ ¹/₂ cup (1 stick/125 g) butter
- ☐ ²/₃ cup (155 g) superfine sugar
- ☐ 1 large potato, cooked and mashed
- ☐ 2 oz (60 g) semisweet (dark) cooking chocolate, melted
- ☐ 3 tablespoons cocoa powder, sifted
- ☐ 2 eggs
- ☐ 1 tablespoon lemon juice
- ☐ 1¹/₂ cups (185 g) all-purpose flour, sifted with 3 teaspoons baking powder, ¹/₂ teaspoon ground nutmeg
- ☐ ²/₃ cup (60 g) walnuts, chopped
- ☐ 3 tablespoons milk

ICING
- ☐ 5 oz (155 g) semisweet (dark) cooking chocolate, melted
- ☐ 1 cup (250 g) dairy sour cream

1   Place butter in a large mixing bowl and beat until light and creamy. Add sugar a little at a time, beating well after each addition. Beat in potato, chocolate, cocoa powder and eggs one at a time. Stir in lemon juice.

2   Combine flour mixture and walnuts. Fold lightly into butter mixture alternately with milk. Spoon mixture into a greased and lined 9-inch (23 cm) round cake pan. Bake at 350°F (180°C) for 35-40 minutes, or until cooked in the center when tested with a skewer. Let stand in pan for 5 minutes before turning out on a wire rack to cool.

3   To make icing: Place chocolate and sour cream in a mixing bowl and beat until combined. Spread over cold cake.

## HONEY BANANA CAKE

Serves 12

- ☐ 1¹/₄ cups (155 g) wholewheat flour
- ☐ 1 cup (125 g) all-purpose flour
- ☐ 3 teaspoons baking powder
- ☐ 1 teaspoon baking soda
- ☐ 1 teaspoon ground nutmeg
- ☐ ³/₄ cup (185 g) raw sugar
- ☐ 2 tablespoons honey, warmed
- ☐ 4 eggs, lightly beaten
- ☐ 5 bananas, mashed
- ☐ 1 cup (250 mL) vegetable oil

HONEY CHEESE TOPPING
- ☐ 4 oz (125 g) cream cheese, softened
- ☐ 2 tablespoons honey
- ☐ ground nutmeg

1   Sift wholewheat and all-purpose flours, baking powder, baking soda and nutmeg into a large mixing bowl. Stir in sugar, honey, eggs, bananas and oil. Beat lightly until smooth.

2   Pour mixture into a greased and lined 9-inch (23 cm) square cake pan. Bake at 325°F (160°C) for 1 hour or until cooked when tested with a skewer. Cool in pan for 10 minutes before turning out onto a wire rack to cool completely.

3   To make topping: Place cream cheese and honey in a bowl and beat until smooth and creamy. Spread over cold cake and sprinkle with nutmeg.

Plates Villeroy & Boch

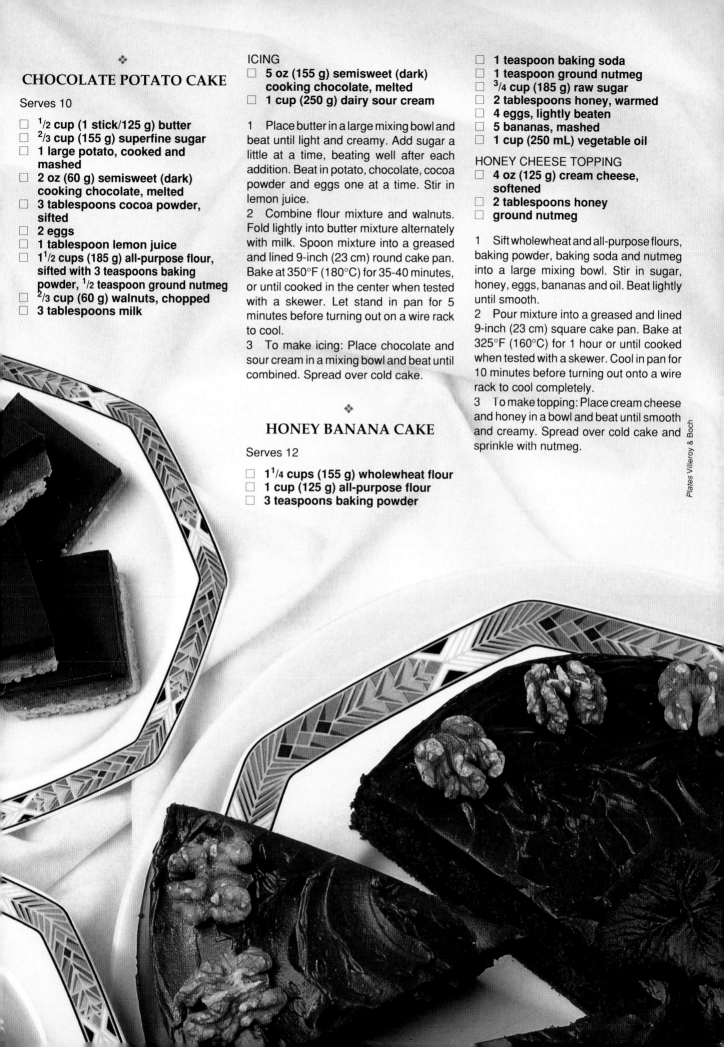

## HERB AND CHEESE MUFFINS

*Perfect for breakfast, brunch or a light snack, these muffins can be frozen and then reheated when required.*

Makes 12-18

- ☐ **2 cups (250 g) all-purpose flour, sifted**
- ☐ **2 tablespoons unprocessed bran**
- ☐ **4 teaspoons baking powder**
- ☐ **1 tablespoon superfine sugar**
- ☐ **¹/₂ cup (60 g) shredded Cheddar cheese**
- ☐ **2 tablespoons mixed chopped fresh herbs, such as parsley, chives or basil**
- ☐ **2 green onions, finely chopped**
- ☐ **¹/₂ cup (1 stick/125 g) poly-unsaturated margarine, melted**
- ☐ **1 egg, lightly beaten**
- ☐ **1 cup (250 mL) milk**

1   Combine flour, bran, baking powder and sugar in a large mixing bowl. Stir in cheese, herbs and green onions.
2   Combine margarine, egg and milk. Add to flour mixture and mix just to combine.
3   Spoon into greased muffin pans, filling two-thirds, and bake at 350°F (180°C) for 25-30 minutes or until golden brown.

❖

## SWEET POTATO BREAD

Serves 10

- ☐ **9¹/₂ oz (300 g) orange-fleshed sweet potato, peeled and shredded**
- ☐ **1¹/₂ cups (250 g) packed brown sugar**
- ☐ **1¹/₂ cups (185 g) all-purpose flour, sifted**
- ☐ **¹/₂ teaspoon ground cinnamon**
- ☐ **1 teaspoon ground nutmeg**
- ☐ **¹/₂ teaspoon vanilla extract**
- ☐ **¹/₂ cup (125 mL) polyunsaturated vegetable oil**
- ☐ **2 eggs, separated**
- ☐ **1 teaspoon baking soda blended with 5 tablespoons water**
- ☐ **1 cup (125 g) chopped almonds**
- ☐ **²/₃ cup (60 g) dry, grated coconut**
- ☐ **²/₃ cup (30 g) shredded coconut**

1   Place sweet potato and half the sugar in a skillet and cook, stirring frequently, for 4-5 minutes. Remove from heat and set aside.
2   Combine flour, cinnamon, nutmeg and remaining sugar in a large bowl. Make a well in the center of the dry ingredients and stir in vanilla, oil, egg yolks and baking soda mixture. Fold in almonds, grated coconut and sweet potato mixture.
3   Beat egg whites until stiff peaks form and fold into cake mixture. Spoon batter into a lightly greased and lined 6 x 10-inch (15 x 25 cm) loaf pan. Sprinkle with shredded coconut and bake at 350°F (180°C) for 1¹/₄ hours, or until cooked when tested. Stand 5 minutes before turning out onto a wire rack to cool.

❖

## SPICY SWEET POTATO AND RAISIN LOAF

Makes 1 loaf

- ☐ **6 oz (185 g) orange-fleshed sweet potato, peeled and roughly chopped**
- ☐ **1 cup (125 g) all-purpose flour**
- ☐ **1 cup (125 g) wholewheat flour**
- ☐ **4 teaspoons baking powder**
- ☐ **¹/₂ teaspoon ground cinnamon**
- ☐ **¹/₂ teaspoon ground ginger**
- ☐ **¹/₂ teaspoon ground nutmeg**
- ☐ **¹/₂ cup (1 stick/125 g) polyunsaturated margarine**
- ☐ **1 cup (125 g) raw sugar**
- ☐ **³/₄ cup (125 g) raisins, chopped**
- ☐ **3 oz (90 mL) milk**
- ☐ **1 egg, lightly beaten**
- ☐ **2 tablespoons vegetable oil**

1   Boil, steam or microwave sweet potato until tender. Drain and place in a food processor or blender and process until smooth. Set aside to cool.
2   Sift flours, baking powder, cinnamon, ginger and nutmeg into a large mixing bowl and return husks to bowl. Rub in margarine with fingertips, then stir in sugar and raisins.
3   Combine milk, egg and oil. Add milk mixture and sweet potato to the flour mixture and mix well to combine. Spread mixture into a greased and lined 4 x 9-inch (10 x 23 cm ) loaf pan. Bake at 350°F (180°C) for 1 hour, or until cooked when tested with a skewer. Cool loaf in pan (tin)

*Herb and Cheese Muffins, Sweet Potato Bread, Spicy Sweet Potato and Raisin Loaf*

*A blanket on the grass, dappled sunshine, a slight breeze and a bulging picnic basket make for a delightful day. Try these ideas for transportable, original, picnic and barbecue food.*

# THE FRESH
## *outdoors*

---

❖
## ROASTED RED PEPPER QUICHES

*These wonderful quiches bring together the flavors of summer.*

Serves 6

- [ ] **16 oz (500 g) prepared or ready-rolled pie crust pastry, thawed**
- [ ] **3 tablespoons grated Parmesan cheese**

FILLING
- [ ] **1 tablespoon (15 g) margarine**
- [ ] **1 onion, thinly sliced**
- [ ] **1 red pepper, roasted and skin removed**
- [ ] **2 eggs**
- [ ] **$^3/_4$ cup (185 mL) light cream**
- [ ] **freshly ground black pepper**
- [ ] **2 tomatoes, peeled, seeded and chopped**
- [ ] **1 tablespoon finely chopped fresh basil**

1  Line six lightly greased individual quiche dishes with pastry. Trim edges and bake blind (see page 86) for 10 minutes at 400°F (200°C). Remove rice and paper, reduce temperature to 350°F (180°C) and bake for 10-15 minutes or until pastry is lightly browned. Set aside to cool.
2  To make filling: Melt margarine in a small skillet and cook onion over medium heat for 5-6 minutes or until soft. Cut pepper into $^1/_2$-inch (1 cm) squares. Place eggs and cream in a bowl and whisk to combine. Season to taste with pepper.
3  Divide onion, tomatoes, basil and pepper between the pastry shells. Spoon over egg mixture and sprinkle with Parmesan cheese. Bake at 350°F (180°C) for 15-20 minutes or until firm.

❖
## RICE TERRINE

Serves 6

- [ ] **$^1/_2$ small head cabbage, separated into leaves and blanched**
- [ ] **$^1/_3$ cup (60 g) wild rice**
- [ ] **1$^1/_3$ cups (200 g) long-grain rice**
- [ ] **2 tablespoons (30 g) margarine**
- [ ] **2 teaspoons ground cumin**
- [ ] **2 teaspoons garam masala**
- [ ] **4 green onions, chopped**
- [ ] **2 stalks celery, finely chopped**
- [ ] **2 eggs, lightly beaten**
- [ ] **1 cup (100 g) shredded Cheddar cheese**
- [ ] **$^1/_3$ cup (60 g) golden raisins**
- [ ] **6$^1/_2$ oz (200 g) canned red peppers, drained and chopped**
- [ ] **freshly ground black pepper**

1  Line a lightly greased 4 x 10-inch (10 x 25 cm) ovenproof loaf pan with cabbage leaves. Allow some of the leaves to overhang the top.
2  Cook wild rice in boiling water for 15 minutes, stir in long-grain rice and cook for 15 minutes longer or until rice is tender. Drain and set aside to cool.
3  Heat margarine in a saucepan and cook cumin, garam masala, green onions and celery for 5 minutes or until celery softens. Remove from heat and set aside.
4  Place rice mixture, celery mixture, eggs, cheese, raisins and red peppers in a large bowl. Season to taste with pepper and mix well to combine. Press into cabbage-lined pan. Fold cabbage leaves over mixture, or use more cabbage leaves to encase filling. Cover with aluminum foil and bake at 400°F (200°C) for 35-40 minutes or until cooked through. Stand for 5 minutes. Turn out and cool completely.

❖
## EGGS WITH FRESH HERB DRESSING

*An attractive salad plate that is perfect for any outing or quick meal. The dressing will keep for several days in the refrigerator and is also great with potato salad.*

Serves 6

- [ ] **lettuce leaves**
- [ ] **6 hard-cooked eggs, peeled and quartered**
- [ ] **12 cherry tomatoes**
- [ ] **1 avocado, pitted, peeled and cut into slices**
- [ ] **24 pitted black olives**

FRESH HERB DRESSING
- [ ] **1 cup (250 g) plain low-fat yogurt**
- [ ] **2 tablespoons chopped fresh parsley**
- [ ] **1 tablespoon chopped fresh mint**
- [ ] **1 tablespoon snipped fresh chives**
- [ ] **2 tablespoons apple juice**
- [ ] **freshly ground black pepper**

1  To make dressing: Place yogurt, parsley, mint, chives and apple juice in a food processor or blender and process until dressing is combined and green in color. Season to taste with pepper.
2  Divide lettuce leaves, eggs, tomatoes, avocado slices and olives between six plates and arrange attractively. To serve: Spoon dressing over, or serve separately.

❖
## SPICED HONEY CREAM AND FRESH FRUIT

Serves 4

- [ ] **1 cup (250 mL) plain low-fat yogurt**
- [ ] **$^1/_2$ cup (125 mL) buttermilk**
- [ ] **$^1/_2$ cup (125 mL) heavy cream**
- [ ] **2 tablespoons honey, warmed**
- [ ] **$^1/_4$ teaspoon ground cinnamon**
- [ ] **$^1/_2$ teaspoon ground nutmeg**
- [ ] **selection roasted nuts**
- [ ] **selection fresh fruit**

Place yogurt, buttermilk, cream, honey, cinnamon and nutmeg in a food processor or blender and process until smooth. Transfer to a bowl, cover and chill. Serve with nuts and fruits.

---

*Spiced Honey Cream and Fresh Fruit, Rice Terrine, Eggs with Fresh Herb Dressing, Roasted Red Pepper Quiches*

*Plates Pillivuyt*

## HERBED HOT DOGS

Serves 6

- [ ] ³/₄ **cup (100 g) peanuts, finely chopped**
- [ ] ³/₄ **cup (100 g) cashew nuts, finely chopped**
- [ ] ³/₄ **cup (100 g) pine nuts, finely chopped**
- [ ] ³/₄ **cup (100 g) sunflower kernels, finely chopped**
- [ ] **1 onion, grated**
- [ ] **1 carrot, peeled and shredded**
- [ ] **1 small red pepper, seeded and finely chopped**
- [ ] **2 teaspoons finely chopped fresh marjoram**
- [ ] **2 teaspoons finely chopped fresh thyme**
- [ ] **2 eggs, lightly beaten**
- [ ] **freshly ground black pepper**
- [ ] **2 oz (60 g) sesame seeds**
- [ ] **vegetable oil for shallow frying**
- [ ] **6 wholewheat bread rolls**
- [ ] **French mustard or catsup**

1   Place peanuts, cashew nuts, pine nuts, sunflower kernels, onion, carrot, pepper, marjoram, thyme and eggs in a bowl and mix well to combine. Season to taste with pepper. Divide into twelve portions and mold each portion into a sausage shape. Roll in sesame seeds.
2   Heat oil in a skillet and cook sausages for 2 minutes each side or until golden. Serve in a bread roll topped with mustard or catsup.

## NUT LOAF

Serves 6

- [ ] **10 oz (315 g) unsalted mixed nuts, finely chopped**
- [ ] ³/₄ **cup (100 g) pine nuts, finely chopped**
- [ ] **1 carrot, peeled and shredded**
- [ ] **1 stalk celery, finely chopped**
- [ ] **1 onion, finely chopped**
- [ ] **1 tomato, peeled and finely chopped**
- [ ] **2 eggs, lightly beaten**
- [ ] **3¹/₂ oz (100 g) wholewheat bread crumbs made from stale bread**
- [ ] **4 oz (125 g) ricotta cheese**
- [ ] **2 teaspoons chopped fresh rosemary**
- [ ] ¹/₂ **cup (125 mL) catsup**
- [ ] **freshly ground black pepper**

1   Combine mixed nuts, pine nuts, carrot, celery, onion, tomato, eggs, bread crumbs, ricotta cheese, rosemary and catsup. Season to taste with pepper.

2   Press mixture into a lightly greased 6 x 10-inch (15 x 25 cm) loaf pan. Bake at 350°F (180°C) for 45 minutes or until firm. Allow to stand for 5 minutes. Turn out to cool.

## SPICED HONEYDEW AND APPLE SOUP

Serves 4

- [ ] **1 honeydew melon, peeled, seeded and cut into chunks**
- [ ] **1¹/₂ cups (375 mL) apple juice**
- [ ] **1 cup (250 mL) dry white wine**
- [ ] **2 teaspoons lemon juice**
- [ ] **1 teaspoon finely chopped ginger preserved in syrup**
- [ ] **small melon balls and mint sprigs**

Place melon in a food processor or blender and process until smooth. Add apple juice, wine, lemon juice and ginger and blend to combine. Transfer to a bowl, cover and refrigerate for 2 hours. Stir occasionally. Garnish with melon balls and mint.

## MARINATED MUSHROOM SALAD

Serves 6

- [ ] **16 oz (500 g) button mushrooms, wiped and stems removed**
- [ ] **2 large red peppers, seeded and sliced**
- [ ] **8 oz (250 g) snow peas, trimmed**

MARINADE
- [ ] **3 tablespoons white vinegar**
- [ ] **3 tablespoons cider vinegar**
- [ ] **3 tablespoons lemon juice**
- [ ] **4 tablespoons olive oil**
- [ ] **1 small red chili, finely chopped**
- [ ] **2 tablespoons tomato paste**
- [ ] **1 tablespoon chopped cilantro (fresh coriander) leaves**
- [ ] **1 tablespoon chopped fresh basil**
- [ ] **2 cloves garlic, crushed**

1   Place mushrooms, peppers and snow peas in a large bowl.
2   To make marinade: Place white and cider vinegars, lemon juice, oil, chili, tomato paste, cilantro, basil and garlic in a screw-top jar. Shake well to combine. Pour over salad and toss to combine. Cover and refrigerate well before serving.

*Herbed Hot Dogs, Nut Loaf, Spiced Honeydew and Apple Soup, Marinated Mushroom Salad*

*Plates Les Olivades Glasses Accoutrement Tiles Pazotti*

## ❖
## INDIAN SWEET POTATO RICE PIE

Serves 4

- ☐ 4 oz (125 g) brown rice, cooked
- ☐ 1 egg, lightly beaten

FILLING

- ☐ 16 oz (500 g) sweet potato, peeled and chopped
- ☐ 1 teaspoon curry paste
- ☐ 1 tablespoon (15 g) margarine
- ☐ 1 teaspoon garam masala
- ☐ 1/2 teaspoon ground coriander
- ☐ 1/2 teaspoon ground cumin
- ☐ 8 oz (250 g) mushrooms, chopped
- ☐ 1 small red pepper, finely chopped
- ☐ 4 green onions, chopped
- ☐ 2 cloves garlic, crushed
- ☐ 1 egg, lightly beaten with 1 tablespoon milk

1   Combine rice and egg and press onto the bottom and up the side of a lightly greased 9-inch (23 cm) pie plate.

2   To make filling: Boil, steam or microwave sweet potato until tender. Drain and mash with curry paste. Set aside to cool. Melt margarine in a saucepan and cook garam masala, coriander, cumin, mushrooms, pepper, green onions and garlic for 10 minutes, or until almost all the liquid has evaporated. Remove from heat and set aside to cool. Mix mushroom and egg mixtures into mashed sweet potato.

3   Spoon filling into pie plate and bake at 350°F (180°C) for 25 minutes or until set.

## ❖
## VEGETABLE KEBABS WITH NUTTY AVOCADO SAUCE

Serves 4

- ☐ 2 zucchini, cut into 1/2-inch (1 cm) pieces
- ☐ 16 button mushrooms
- ☐ 1 red pepper, seeded and cut into 1-inch (2.5 cm) cubes
- ☐ 4 canned pineapple slices, each cut into 8 pieces

GLAZE

- ☐ 3 tablespoons olive oil
- ☐ 1 tablespoon balsamic vinegar
- ☐ 1 teaspoon chopped fresh basil
- ☐ 1 clove garlic, crushed
- ☐ 1 teaspoon grated lime rind
- ☐ freshly ground black pepper

NUTTY AVOCADO SAUCE

- ☐ 1 small ripe avocado, pitted, peeled and roughly chopped
- ☐ 3 tablespoons plain low-fat yogurt
- ☐ 1 tablespoon lemon juice
- ☐ 2 tablespoons finely chopped walnuts
- ☐ 2 teaspoons cider vinegar
- ☐ pinch cayenne pepper

1   Thread zucchini, mushrooms, pepper and pineapple alternately onto eight greased wooden skewers.

2   To make glaze: Place oil, vinegar, basil, garlic, lime rind and pepper to taste in a bowl. Whisk to combine and brush over kebabs. Broil or barbecue kebabs for 8-10 minutes, or until vegetables are tender. Turn and brush with remaining glaze halfway through cooking.

3   To make sauce: Place avocado, yogurt, lemon juice, walnuts, vinegar and cayenne in a food processor or blender and process until smooth. Serve with kebabs.

Plates Taitu Basket Mosmania

## WHAT SIZE?

What is the difference between cubing, dicing, grinding and slicing?

The following guide will help you understand what is meant by the different terms used in a recipe:

**Cube:** cut into about $1/2$-inch (1 cm) pieces.

**Dice:** cut into pieces about half the size of cube.

**Grind:** cut into very small pieces in a mincer or food processor.

**Grate:** use either a hand grater or a food processor with a grating attachment.

**Shred:** use a hand grater or a food processor with a shredding attachment to make long narrow strips.

**Slice:** can be any size ranging from very thin to thick. You can also slice into rings. Another way to slice is to cut diagonally. This is a good way to prepare vegetables such as carrots, celery and zucchini for stir-frying.

# MARINATED EGGPLANT AND TOMATO SALAD

*Using basil, garlic and balsamic vinegar, this salad combines the flavors of Italy. Serve as a starter, as part of an antipasto platter or take it on a picnic. It is delicious served with pita bread and yogurt.*

Serves 6

- ☐ **6 baby eggplants, cut lengthwise into $1/2$-inch (1 cm) slices**
- ☐ **olive oil**
- ☐ **3 tomatoes, peeled and thinly sliced**
- ☐ **4 tablespoons finely chopped fresh basil**
- ☐ **freshly ground black pepper**

DRESSING
- ☐ **3 tablespoons balsamic vinegar**
- ☐ **1 tablespoon olive oil**
- ☐ **2 cloves garlic, crushed**

1   Brush each eggplant slice generously with olive oil and broil under a preheated broiler for 4-5 minutes on each side or until golden and tender.

2   To make dressing, place vinegar, oil and garlic in a screw-top jar. Shake well to combine.

3   Place a layer of warm eggplant slices in a shallow ceramic or glass dish. Top with a layer of tomato slices. Sprinkle with a tablespoon of dressing, a tablespoon of basil and season with pepper. Repeat layers until all eggplant and tomatoes are used. Cover and refrigerate for at least 2 hours.

---

### COOK'S TIP

If the eggplant appears to be drying out during cooking, brush with a little more olive oil. This salad is even better if left to marinate overnight.

---

*Left: Indian Sweet Potato Rice Pie,*
*Vegetable Kebabs with Nutty Avocado Sauce*
*Above: Spicy Pea Parathas (page 62),*
*Marinated Eggplant and Tomato Salad*

61

*Salad Bowl Mosmania*

DRESSING
- [ ] **1 tablespoon olive oil**
- [ ] **1 teaspoon grated lime rind**
- [ ] **2 tablespoons lime juice**
- [ ] **1 teaspoon coarse grain mustard**
- [ ] **1 tablespoon honey**
- [ ] **1 tablespoon chopped fresh basil**

1   Bring vegetable stock to the boil and pour over couscous. Set aside to stand for 10 minutes, then drain.

2   Combine couscous, carrot, pepper, tomato, cucumber and avocado in a bowl.

3   To make dressing: Place oil, rind, juice, mustard, honey and basil in a screwtop jar. Shake well to combine. Pour over salad and toss. Just before serving sprinkle with almonds.

❖

## CRUNCHY HONEY AND DATE SLICE

- [ ] **²/₃ cup (90 g) rolled oats**
- [ ] **¹/₂ cup (60 g) all-purpose flour, sifted**
- [ ] **3¹/₂ oz (100 g) dry grated coconut**
- [ ] **1¹/₂ cups (45 g) corn flakes, lightly crushed**
- [ ] **3 oz (90 g) raw sugar**
- [ ] **1 cup (155 g) chopped dried dates**
- [ ] **¹/₂ cup (125 g) margarine**
- [ ] **3 tablespoons honey**

CHOCOLATE ICING
- [ ] **¹/₃ cup (90 g) margarine**
- [ ] **1¹/₂ cups (250 g) IOX (confectioners') sugar, sifted**
- [ ] **1 tablespoon cocoa powder, sifted**
- [ ] **2 tablespoons light cream**

---

## SPICY PEA PARATHAS

*You may like to serve these with a spicy tomato sauce.*

Serves 4

- [ ] **2 cups (250 g) wholewheat flour**
- [ ] **2 cups (250 g) all-purpose flour**
- [ ] **2 tablespoons (30 g) margarine**
- [ ] **1 cup (250 mL) warm water, approximately**

FILLING
- [ ] **1 large potato, cooked and mashed**
- [ ] **3 tablespoons (45 g) split peas, cooked and mashed**
- [ ] **4 oz (125 g) ricotta cheese**
- [ ] **2 teaspoons coriander seeds**
- [ ] **2 teaspoons cumin seeds**
- [ ] **1¹/₂ tablespoons sweet fruit chutney**

1   Sift wholewheat and all-purpose flours into a large bowl. Rub in margarine, make a well in the center and gradually add enough water to form a soft dough. Knead on a lightly floured surface until smooth.

2   To make filling: Place potato, split peas, ricotta cheese, coriander and cumin seeds, and chutney in a bowl. Mix well to combine.

3   Divide dough into eight portions and roll into small flat rounds. Place a spoonful of filling in the center of each round. Mold dough around filling to enclose.

4   Cook parathas on a lightly greased barbecue plate, or in a skillet, for 4 minutes on each side or until golden.

❖

## COUSCOUS SALAD

*With a tasty dressing that has the added piquancy of lime, this salad would be perfect for your next al fresco meal.*

Serves 4

- [ ] **1 cup (250 mL) vegetable stock, broth or water**
- [ ] **6¹/₂ oz (200 g) couscous**
- [ ] **1 carrot, peeled and thinly sliced**
- [ ] **1 red pepper, chopped**
- [ ] **1 tomato, chopped**
- [ ] **1 small cucumber, peeled and cubed**
- [ ] **1 avocado, peeled, pitted and cubed**
- [ ] **¹/₄ cup (30 g) slivered almonds, toasted**

---

### COUSCOUS

✧  Couscous is a fine semolina made from wheat that originated in North Africa. Variations on the traditional dish, however, can be found in Sicily, France and even Brazil, where it is cuscuz rather than couscous.

✧  It is readily available in packages, much the same as rice, and is served as an accompaniment to a meal.

✧  The name couscous applies both to the uncooked granules and the finished dish.

✧  Cold couscous is a pleasantly bland background for vegetable salads and is particularly delicious when dressed with tart lemon or lime dressing.

1   Place oats, flour, coconut, corn flakes and sugar in a large bowl. Combine dates, margarine and honey in a saucepan and stir over low heat until margarine melts. Bring to the boil, remove from heat. Stir honey mixture into dry ingredients and mix well.

2   Press mixture into a greased and lined 7 x 11-inch (18 x 28 cm) shallow cake pan. Bake at 350°F (180°C) for 20-25 minutes or until golden. Cool layer in pan before turning out.

3   To make icing: Beat margarine in a small bowl until creamy. Add confectioners' sugar, cocoa powder and cream. Beat until icing is a spreadable consistency. Spread over cold layer, allow to set and then cut into fingers.

❖

## TANGY APPLE AND APRICOT LOAF

*An easily prepared moist loaf that is great for picnics and lunch boxes.*

Makes 1 loaf

- [ ] **$2^1/_3$ cups (155 g) dried apricots, chopped**
- [ ] **2 cups (125 g) dried apples, chopped**
- [ ] **2 teaspoons grated lemon rind**
- [ ] **2 tablespoons lemon juice**
- [ ] **$^2/_3$ cup (170 mL) water**
- [ ] **1 cup (185 g) packed brown sugar**
- [ ] **$^1/_4$ cup (60 g) margarine**
- [ ] **$1^1/_3$ cups (185 g) wholewheat flour, sifted**
- [ ] **$^1/_2$ cup (60 g) all-purpose flour, sifted with 3 teaspoons baking powder**

1   Place apricots, apples, lemon rind, lemon juice, water, sugar and margarine in a saucepan. Bring to the boil and simmer for 5 minutes. Remove from heat and set aside to cool for 5 minutes.

2   Stir wholewheat and all-purpose flours and baking powder into fruit mixture. Spread mixture into a greased and lined 5 x 9-inch (12 x 23 cm) loaf pan. Bake at 350°F (180°C) for 1 hour, or until center is cooked when tested with a skewer. Cool loaf in pan for 15 minutes before turning out onto a wire rack to cool completely.

*Left: Couscous Salad*
*Right: Tangy Apple and Apricot Loaf, Crunchy Honey and Date Slice*

Plates Accoutrement *Silverware* Whitehill Silver

*"Christmas is coming, the vegetables are getting fat."*
*Well no, it doesn't sound quite right, but there is no*
*reason why those who choose not to eat meat should*
*miss out on sharing the good flavors.*

# CHRISTMAS FARE
## *with traditional flavor*

❖

### SPICY CHRISTMAS NUTS

*These nuts are baked rather than fried.*

Serves 10

- ☐ **2 teaspoons ground coriander**
- ☐ **1 teaspoon ground cumin**
- ☐ **1 teaspoon garam masala**
- ☐ **¹/₂ teaspoon cayenne pepper**
- ☐ **¹/₂ teaspoon ground ginger**
- ☐ **freshly ground black pepper**
- ☐ **1¹/₂ cups (250 g) whole almonds, blanched**
- ☐ **4 oz (125 g) unsalted cashews**
- ☐ **1¹/₄ cups (125 g) walnut halves**
- ☐ **1 egg white, lightly beaten**

1 Combine coriander, cumin, garam masala, cayenne pepper, ginger and pepper and place in a shallow dish. Place almonds, cashews and walnuts in a bowl. Add egg white and toss to coat nuts. Remove with a slotted spoon, then roll in spice mixture.
2 Place on a cookie sheet and bake at 250°F (120°C) for 1 hour or until the nuts are dry. Set aside to cool.

---

### FRESH CHESTNUTS

❖ If fresh chestnuts are available they can be used to make the Spicy Chestnut and Apple Soup.

❖ To prepare chestnuts for use, make a small nick in the flat side of each chestnut. Place in a saucepan and cover with cold water, bring to the boil, then remove pan from heat. Remove chestnuts from water one at a time and cut off the shells and remove the inner skin. When this starts to become difficult, return the pan to the heat and bring back to the boil. Repeat process until all chestnuts are shelled.

❖

### SPICY CHESTNUT AND APPLE SOUP

Serves 10

- ☐ **2 tablespoons (30 g) margarine**
- ☐ **2 large onions, finely chopped**
- ☐ **1 clove garlic, crushed**
- ☐ **2 green apples, peeled, cored and roughly chopped**
- ☐ **¹/₂ teaspoon ground coriander**
- ☐ **¹/₂ teaspoon ground cumin**
- ☐ **¹/₂ teaspoon chili powder**
- ☐ **14 oz (440 g) canned chestnuts, drained, rinsed and roughly chopped**
- ☐ **7¹/₂ cups (1.8 litres) vegetable stock or broth**
- ☐ **1 cup (250 mL) light cream**
- ☐ **2 tablespoons dry sherry (optional)**
- ☐ **freshly ground black pepper**

1 Melt margarine in a large saucepan and cook onions, garlic and apples over medium heat for 5-6 minutes or until onion softens. Stir in coriander, cumin and chili powder and cook for 1 minute longer.
2 Add chestnuts and stock to pan, bring to the boil and simmer for 30 minutes. Remove pan from heat and set aside to cool for 15 minutes. Transfer soup to food processor or blender and process until smooth. Return soup to a clean pan, stir in cream and heat gently. Just before serving, stir in sherry and season to taste with pepper.

*Clockwise from left: Spicy Chestnut and Apple Soup, Christmas Koulibiaca (page 66), Spicy Christmas Nuts, Minced Fruit Pie (page 67), Blue Cheese Quiches with Cranberry Sauce (page 66), Watercress and Goat Cheese Salad (page 67), Three-Rice Salad Wrapped in Leaves (page 66)*

*Plates Villeroy & Boch Glasses Saywell Silverware Whitehill Silver*

## CHRISTMAS KOULIBIACA

*A flavorsome dish. Make the fillings the day before, and scoop the center from the loaf earlier in the day, leaving just the filling and final baking prior to your dinner.*

Serves 10

- ☐ **1 loaf wholegrain bread**

STUFFING LAYER
- ☐ **$1/4$ cup (60 g) margarine**
- ☐ **1 onion, finely chopped**
- ☐ **$1/2$ teaspoon dried rosemary**
- ☐ **$1/2$ teaspoon dried thyme**
- ☐ **$1/2$ teaspoon dried oregano**
- ☐ **bread crumbs (see method)**
- ☐ **freshly ground black pepper**

TOMATO LAYER
- ☐ **1 tablespoon vegetable oil**
- ☐ **1 large onion, sliced**
- ☐ **1 clove garlic, crushed**
- ☐ **1 small red chili, seeded and finely chopped**
- ☐ **14 oz (440 g) canned peeled tomatoes, mashed and undrained**
- ☐ **freshly ground black pepper**
- ☐ **1 tablespoon chopped fresh basil**

SPINACH LAYER
- ☐ **16 oz (500 g) spinach, stems removed and leaves chopped**
- ☐ **8 oz (250 g) ricotta cheese**
- ☐ **1 tablespoon grated Parmesan cheese**
- ☐ **pinch ground nutmeg**
- ☐ **freshly ground black pepper**

EGGPLANT LAYER
- ☐ **1 small eggplant**
- ☐ **1 tablespoon vegetable oil**
- ☐ **1 large onion, chopped**
- ☐ **2 tablespoons (30 g) margarine**
- ☐ **2 oz (60 g) button mushrooms, sliced**
- ☐ **freshly ground black pepper**

1   Cut a slice from top of loaf of bread and scoop out center leaving a shell approximately $1/2$-inch (1 cm) thick. Reserve bread crumbs for stuffing. Set loaf and lid aside.

2   To make stuffing: Melt margarine in a skillet and cook onion, rosemary, thyme and oregano for 4-5 minutes, or until onion softens. Mix with bread crumbs and season to taste with pepper. Set aside.

3   To make tomato layer: Heat oil in a skillet and cook onion, garlic and chili for 5 minutes, or until onion softens. Stir in tomatoes and simmer for 30 minutes, or until a very thick tomato sauce forms.

Season to taste with pepper and stir in basil. Set aside to cool.

4   To make spinach layer: Steam, microwave or pan-cook spinach leaves until wilted. Drain and set aside to cool. Using your hands, squeeze as much liquid as possible from spinach and chop. Place spinach, ricotta, Parmesan cheese and nutmeg in a bowl. Mix to combine and season to taste with pepper. Set aside.

5   To make eggplant layer: Bake eggplant in oven at 350°F (180°C) for 40 minutes or until tender. Remove from oven and set aside until cool enough to handle. Peel and mash eggplant. Heat oil in a skillet and cook onion for 5 minutes or until soft. Remove onion from pan and drain on paper towels. Melt margarine in skillet and cook mushrooms for 3-4 minutes or until just tender. Remove mushrooms and drain on paper towels. Place eggplant in a bowl. Add onions, mushrooms, 2 tablespoons stuffing and pepper to taste. Mix to combine.

6   To assemble koulibiaca: Spoon eggplant filling into base of shell and smooth top using a spatula. Spoon over one-third of stuffing, then top with spinach filling and smooth top. Spoon over another one-third of stuffing, then tomato mixture and finally remaining stuffing. Replace lid and bake at 350°F (180°C) for 1 hour or until heated through. If top starts to brown too much during cooking, cover with aluminum foil. Serve koulibiaca hot, cut into slices, with Rich Tomato Sauce (see recipe page 85).

❖

## BLUE CHEESE QUICHES WITH CRANBERRY SAUCE

Serves 10

- ☐ **12 oz (375 g) ready-rolled puff pastry, thawed**
- ☐ **2 tablespoons (30 g) margarine**
- ☐ **2 onions, thinly sliced**

FILLING
- ☐ **6 eggs**
- ☐ **9 oz (280 mL) light cream**
- ☐ **9 oz (280 mL) milk**
- ☐ **freshly ground black pepper**
- ☐ **$1^1/2$ cups (185 g) blue cheese, crumbled**

CRANBERRY SAUCE
- ☐ **8 oz (250 g) canned cranberry sauce**
- ☐ **$1/2$ cup (125 mL) port or red wine**
- ☐ **$1/2$ teaspoon ground allspice**
- ☐ **2 teaspoons cornstarch blended with 4 tablespoons water**

1   Line ten greased 5-inch (12 cm) individual quiche pans with pastry. Melt margarine in a small skillet and cook onions for 10 minutes or until soft and golden. Divide into ten portions and spread over bottoms of quiches.

2   To make filling: Place eggs, cream, milk and pepper in a bowl and mix to combine. Stir in cheese, spoon mixture into quiches and bake at 400°F (200°C) for 25-30 minutes or until firm and golden.

3   To make sauce: Place cranberry sauce, port and allspice in a saucepan, bring to the boil, then reduce heat and simmer for 5 minutes. Stir in cornstarch mixture and cook until sauce thickens. Serve with hot or warm quiches.

❖

## THREE-RICE SALAD WRAPPED IN LEAVES

Serves 10

- ☐ **10 large lettuce leaves, blanched**

RICE SALAD
- ☐ **4 oz (125 g) long-grain wild rice, cooked**
- ☐ **4 oz (125 g) short-grain brown rice, cooked**
- ☐ **4 oz (125 g) white rice, cooked**
- ☐ **2 green onions, finely chopped**
- ☐ **1 tablespoon finely snipped fresh chives**
- ☐ **1 tablespoon finely chopped fresh mint**
- ☐ **1 tablespoon finely chopped fresh parsley**
- ☐ **1 green apple, cored and finely chopped**
- ☐ **3 tablespoons slivered almonds, toasted**
- ☐ **freshly ground black pepper**

DRESSING
- ☐ **1 clove garlic, crushed**
- ☐ **2 tablespoons olive oil**
- ☐ **2 tablespoons balsamic vinegar**
- ☐ **1 tablespoon fresh lime juice**

1   To make salad: Place wild, brown and white rices, green onions, chives, mint, parsley, apple and almonds in a bowl and toss to combine.

2   To make dressing: Place garlic, oil, vinegar and lime juice in a screwtop jar and shake well to combine. Pour over salad and season to taste with pepper. Toss to coat all ingredients with dressing.

3   Place a spoonful of salad in center of each lettuce leaf. Fold leaf around salad to form a parcel.

## WATERCRESS AND GOAT CHEESE SALAD

Serves 6

- ☐ 1 bunch watercress
- ☐ 1 Bibb or Boston lettuce, washed and leaves separated
- ☐ 2 oz (60 g) hazelnuts, roughly chopped

HAZELNUT DRESSING
- ☐ 2 tablespoons hazelnut oil
- ☐ 4 tablespoons white wine vinegar
- ☐ 1 teaspoon Dijon-style mustard
- ☐ freshly ground black pepper

CROUTONS
- ☐ 4 oz (125 g) goat cheese
- ☐ 1 clove garlic, crushed
- ☐ 2 tablespoons finely snipped fresh chives
- ☐ 4 slices wholewheat bread, toasted on one side

1   To make dressing: Place oil, vinegar and mustard in a screw top jar and shake well to combine. Season to taste with pepper. Combine watercress and lettuce in a bowl and toss with dressing. Arrange salad on six plates. Sprinkle with hazelnuts and set aside.

2   To make croutons: Mash cheese, garlic and chives together and spread over untoasted side of bread. Cut bread into 1-inch (2.5 cm) cubes and broil under a preheated broiler for 5 minutes, or until cheese is melted and golden. Top salad with hot croutons and serve immediately.

❖

## MINCED FRUIT PIE

*Minced fruit pies originally were a mixture of minced or shredded meat, dried fruits and spices. By the end of the nineteenth century the meat was omitted and the mince pie as we know it today was born.*

Serves 10

- ☐ 1 egg, lightly beaten with 1 tablespoon water
- ☐ 1/3 cup (60 g) IOX (confectioners') sugar, sifted

PASTRY
- ☐ 1/2 cup (125 g) polyunsaturated margarine, softened
- ☐ 1/4 cup (60 g) superfine sugar
- ☐ 1 egg
- ☐ 2 teaspoons milk
- ☐ 2 cups (250 g) all-purpose flour
- ☐ 1 teaspoon baking powder

FILLING
- ☐ 1/2 cup (125 mL) apple juice
- ☐ 1/2 cup (90 g) packed brown sugar
- ☐ 1 green apple, peeled, cored and roughly chopped
- ☐ 1 pear, peeled, cored and roughly chopped
- ☐ 1/2 cup (60 g) dried apricots, chopped
- ☐ 3/4 cup (125 g) currants
- ☐ 3/4 cup (125 g) golden raisins
- ☐ 1/3 cup (60 g) chopped dried figs
- ☐ 2 tablespoons (30 g) candied cherries, chopped
- ☐ 1/4 cup (30 g) finely chopped almonds
- ☐ 1/4 cup (30 g) finely chopped hazelnuts
- ☐ 1/2 teaspoon ground nutmeg
- ☐ 1/2 teaspoon ground cinnamon
- ☐ 1/4 teaspoon ground mixed spice
- ☐ 1 tablespoon lemon juice
- ☐ 1 tablespoon orange juice
- ☐ 1 teaspoon grated lemon rind
- ☐ 1 teaspoon grated orange rind
- ☐ 2 tablespoons brandy

1   To make filling: Place apple juice and sugar in a large saucepan and cook over low heat for 4-5 minutes, or until sugar dissolves. Stir in apple, pear, apricots, currants, raisins, figs, cherries, almonds, hazelnuts, nutmeg, cinnamon, mixed spice, lemon and orange juices, lemon and orange rinds and brandy. Bring slowly to the boil, stirring constantly. Reduce heat, cover and simmer gently, stirring occasionally, for 25-30 minutes, or until fruit mixture is a soft pulp. Remove pan from heat and set aside to cool completely.

2   To make pastry: Place margarine and sugar in a bowl and beat until light and fluffy. Mix in egg and milk. Sift together flour and baking powder and add to egg mixture, mixing to form a dough. Turn out onto a lightly floured surface. Roll out three-quarters of the pastry to line a lightly greased 10-inch (25 cm) pie dish (plate). Trim edges and bake blind at 400°F (200°C) for 10 minutes. Remove rice and paper and reduce heat to 350°F (180°C). Bake for 12-15 minutes longer, or until pastry is light golden. Set aside to cool.

3   Spread filling over pastry shell. Roll out remaining pastry and cut into 1/2-inch (1 cm) strips and arrange in a lattice pattern on top of fruit. Brush pastry with egg mixture and bake at 400°F (200°C) for 15-20 minutes, or until pastry is golden and filling hot. Serve warm or at room temperature. Just before serving, sprinkle with confectioners' sugar.

---

## CHRISTMAS SPIRIT

Christmas is a time for entertaining, and these drinks will ensure that any entertaining you do will go off with a real bang.

❖

### EGGNOG

*Eggnog is a traditional Christmas eve or morning drink. If you wish, you can make it without the rum and brandy. Just increase the amount of cream and milk you use.*

Serves 10

- ☐ 5 eggs
- ☐ 1 cup (250 mL) milk
- ☐ 1 cup (250 mL) light cream
- ☐ 1 cup (250 mL) dark rum
- ☐ 1 cup (250 mL) brandy
- ☐ 4 tablespoons superfine sugar
- ☐ 2 teaspoons vanilla extract
- ☐ ice cubes
- ☐ ground (grated) nutmeg

Place eggs, milk, cream, rum, brandy, sugar and vanilla in a food processor or blender and process to combine. Place ice cubes in glasses and pour over eggnog. Dust with nutmeg and serve.

❖

### MULLED WINE

*In Saxon times and for many centuries, it was customary to have the wassail bowl steaming throughout the Christmas period. This is the modern day version, and is fun to serve to your guests at this festive time of year.*

Serves 10

- ☐ 12 sugar cubes
- ☐ strips lemon rind
- ☐ strips orange rind
- ☐ 6 cloves
- ☐ 1 cinnamon stick
- ☐ 1 cup (250 mL) cold water
- ☐ 2 bottles dry red wine

1   Place sugar cubes, lemon and orange rinds, cloves, cinnamon stick and water in saucepan. Bring to the boil and cook until sugar dissolves.

2   Add wine and bring to just below boiling point. Strain into a warm jug and serve in warmed glasses.

*Those interested in following a healthier eating pattern no longer need to turn down the final course. The honeys, berries, nuts and yogurts of this world – all good for you – can be combined into some fabulous treats.*

# RICH REWARDS
## *sweet treats*

❖

### PASSIONFRUIT MOUSSE WITH ORANGE SAUCE

*Ricotta and reduced-fat cream make this a not-so-wicked dessert for the weight-conscious cook. The Orange Sauce is a perfect alternative to cream.*

Serves 6

- ☐ 6$^1$/$_2$ oz (200 g) ricotta cheese
- ☐ $^1$/$_2$ cup (125 mL) reduced-fat cream
- ☐ 2 tablespoons IOX (confectioners') sugar
- ☐ 1 tablespoon gelatin dissolved in 2 tablespoons hot water
- ☐ $^1$/$_4$ cup (60 mL) passionfruit pulp
- ☐ 3 egg whites

ORANGE SAUCE
- ☐ 6$^1$/$_2$ fl oz (200 mL) fresh orange juice, strained
- ☐ 3$^1$/$_2$ oz (100 mL) clear apple juice
- ☐ 2 tablespoons sugar
- ☐ 2 teaspoons cornstarch blended with 2 tablespoons water

1  Place ricotta, cream and confectioners' sugar in a food processor or blender and process until smooth. Stir in gelatin mixture and passionfruit pulp. Mix well. Whisk egg whites until soft peaks form and then fold into fruit mixture. Spoon mixture into six $^1$/$_2$-cup (125 mL) capacity, moistened molds. Refrigerate until set.
2  To make sauce: Combine orange juice, apple juice and sugar in a saucepan and cook over low heat, stirring frequently, until sugar dissolves. Bring to the boil, then reduce heat and simmer for 3 minutes. Stir in cornstarch mixture and cook over medium heat, stirring frequently, until sauce boils and thickens. Remove from heat and set aside to cool. Refrigerate sauce until well chilled. Turn out molds and serve with sauce.

❖

### STRAWBERRY AND ALMOND TOFU SURPRISE

*A wonderfully light summer dessert with a smooth texture. Served in slices with fresh berries and toasted coconut, it makes an extra special finale for a dinner party.*

Serves 8

- ☐ 1$^1$/$_4$ cups (185 g) whole almonds, toasted
- ☐ 2 tablespoons dry grated coconut, toasted

FILLING
- ☐ 6$^1$/$_2$ oz (200 g) strawberries, hulled and roughly chopped
- ☐ 9$^1$/$_2$ oz (300 g) soft tofu
- ☐ $^1$/$_2$ cup (125 mL) coconut milk
- ☐ $^1$/$_2$ cup (125 g) superfine sugar

1  Place almonds and coconut in a food processor or blender and process until evenly chopped. Sprinkle half the nut mixture over the bottom of a greased and foil-lined 7-inch (18 cm) springform pan.
2  To make filling: Place strawberries, tofu, coconut milk and sugar in a food processor or blender and process until smooth. Pour mixture carefully over nuts in pan. Sprinkle remaining nut mixture evenly over filling and freeze until firm.

*Strawberry and Almond Tofu Surprise, Lime and Coconut Baked Custard, Passionfruit Mousse with Orange Sauce*

*Silverware Whitehill Silver Tiles Pazotti*

❖

# LIME AND COCONUT BAKED CUSTARD

Serves 6

- ☐ **3 eggs**
- ☐ **4 egg yolks**
- ☐ **³/₄ cup (185 g) superfine sugar**
- ☐ **1¹/₂ cups (375 mL) coconut milk**
- ☐ **¹/₂ cup (125 mL) light cream**
- ☐ **1 cup (250 mL) milk**
- ☐ **4 cups (375 g) dry grated coconut**
- ☐ **2 tablespoons grated lime rind**
- ☐ **ground nutmeg for dusting**
- ☐ **toasted shredded coconut**
- ☐ **lime rind for garnishing**

1 Beat eggs, egg yolks, and sugar in a bowl until light and fluffy.

2 Combine coconut milk, cream and milk in a saucepan and heat until almost boiling. Remove from heat and set aside to cool slightly. Gradually pour milk mixture into egg mixture and beat until combined. Mix in coconut and lime rind.

3 Pour custard into a buttered 1 pint (600 mL) baking dish. Stand dish in a baking pan and add enough boiling water to come halfway up the sides of the dish. Bake at 350°F (180°C) for 1 hour or until set.

4 Remove from oven. Dust with nutmeg and decorate with shredded coconut and lime rind. Serve warm.

## WHEATY PEACH AND MANGO CRUMBLE

Serves 8

- ☐ **14 oz (440 g) canned mango slices, drained**
- ☐ **14 oz (440 g) canned peach slices, drained**

FILLING
- ☐ **6$^1$/$_2$ oz (200 g) peach and mango low-fat yogurt**
- ☐ **2 tablespoons dairy sour cream**
- ☐ **2 eggs, separated**
- ☐ **$^1$/$_4$ cup (60 g) sugar**
- ☐ **2 teaspoons all-purpose flour**

TOPPING
- ☐ **$^3$/$_4$ cup (90 g) wholewheat flour**
- ☐ **$^1$/$_2$ cup finely crushed wheat flake breakfast cereal (Weet-a-Bix)**
- ☐ **2 tablespoons dry grated coconut**
- ☐ **4 tablespoons packed brown sugar**
- ☐ **1 teaspoon grated lemon rind**
- ☐ **$^1$/$_3$ cup (90 g) margarine, melted**

1  Arrange mango and peach slices over the bottom of a shallow baking dish.
2  To make filling: Place yogurt, sour cream, egg yolks, sugar and flour in a bowl and mix well to combine. Beat egg whites until soft peaks form, then fold in yogurt mixture and pour over fruit.
3  To make topping: Place flour, crushed cereal, coconut, sugar, lemon rind and margarine in a bowl and mix well. Sprinkle evenly over filling and bake at 350°F (180°C) for 30 minutes, or until filling is set and topping browned.

### SOUFFLE COLLARS

Cut a piece of waxed paper 2 inches (5 cm) longer than the circumference of the soufflé dish. Fold in half lengthwise to give a double thickness. Brush with melted butter and sprinkle with dry bread crumbs for a savory soufflé, or superfine sugar for a sweet soufflé. Wrap the collar around the soufflé dish. The soufflé dish should also be greased and sprinkled with bread crumbs or sugar – the collar should extend 2 inches (5 cm) above the rim of the dish. Tie in place with string.

## CARROT AND LIME SOUFFLES

Serves 6

- ☐ **3 carrots, peeled and roughly chopped**
- ☐ **3 eggs**
- ☐ **$^2$/$_3$ cup (155 g) superfine sugar**
- ☐ **3 teaspoons gelatin dissolved in 1 tablespoon Cointreau and 1 tablespoon lime juice**
- ☐ **1 teaspoon grated lime rind**
- ☐ **1 cup (250 mL) heavy cream, whipped**

1  Boil, steam or microwave carrots until tender. Drain and place in a food processor or blender and process until smooth. Set aside to cool.
2  Place eggs and sugar in a mixing bowl and beat until thick and creamy – this will take about 10 minutes. Fold in gelatin mixture, rind, cream and carrot purée.
3  Spoon mixture into six individual soufflé dishes with a 1$^1$/$_4$-inch (3 cm) high foil collar attached. Refrigerate until firm. Remove collar and serve.

## HONEY AND CARROT RICOTTA ROLL

*This carrot roll makes a delightful change from the better known carrot cake.*

Serves 8

- [ ] **4 eggs, separated**
- [ ] **¹/₂ cup (125 g) superfine sugar**
- [ ] **¹/₂ cup (60 g) all-purpose flour**
- [ ] **1 teaspoon ground cinnamon**
- [ ] **1 teaspoon ground nutmeg**
- [ ] **1 teaspoon ground allspice**
- [ ] **1 large carrot, peeled and shredded**
- [ ] **2 tablespoons honey**
- [ ] **IOX (confectioners') sugar**

FILLING
- [ ] **1 cup (125 g) dried apricots, chopped**
- [ ] **¹/₂ cup (125 mL) brandy**
- [ ] **8 oz (250 g) ricotta or cottage cheese**
- [ ] **¹/₂ cup (125 g) plain low-fat yogurt**
- [ ] **1 tablespoon honey**
- [ ] **1 teaspoon ground nutmeg**
- [ ] **2 tablespoons slivered almonds**

1   Place egg yolks and sugar in a bowl and beat until pale and thick. Sift together flour, cinnamon, nutmeg and allspice. Fold flour mixture and carrot into egg yolks. Whisk egg whites until soft peaks form. Gradually add honey and continue to beat until stiff peaks form. Fold into carrot mixture.

2   Spoon batter carefully into a greased and lined 10 x 12-inch (25 x 30 cm) jelly (Swiss) roll pan. Bake at 350°F (180°C) for 15-20 minutes or until firm to touch.

3   When roll is cooked, turn out quickly onto a tea towel or sheet of baking paper sprinkled with superfine sugar, and roll up from the short end like a jelly (Swiss) roll. Stand until cold.

4   To make filling: Soak apricots in brandy for at least 1 hour. Place ricotta cheese, yogurt, honey and nutmeg in the food processor or blender and process until smooth. Drain apricots. Fold apricots and almonds through ricotta mixture.

5   Unroll cake when cold and remove baking paper. Spread cake with filling and roll again. Just before serving, sprinkle with sifted confectioners' sugar.

## ALMOND AND GINGER TREATS

Serves 4

- [ ] **3 teaspoons gelatin**
- [ ] **6 oz (185 mL) water**
- [ ] **¹/₂ cup (125 g) sugar**
- [ ] **6 oz (185 mL) boiling water**
- [ ] **1¹/₄ cups (300 mL) milk**
- [ ] **2 drops almond extract**
- [ ] **2 kiwifruit, peeled and sliced**
- [ ] **¹/₃ cup (60 g) candied (glacé) ginger, finely chopped**
- [ ] **ground nutmeg**

1   Sprinkle gelatin over cold water and stir in sugar. Pour in boiling water and stir until sugar and gelatin dissolve.

2   Stir in milk and almond extract. Pour mixture into four individual serving dishes. Set aside to cool, then refrigerate until set. To serve: Decorate with kiwifruit and ginger and sprinkle with nutmeg.

*Carrot and Lime Soufflés, Wheaty Peach and Mango Crumble, Honey and Carrot Ricotta Roll, Almond and Ginger Treats*

Plates Incorporated Agencies

## SPICY PUMPKIN AND PRUNE SOUFFLE

Serves 4

- ☐ 3¹/₂ tablespoons superfine sugar
- ☐ 1 teaspoon vanilla extract
- ☐ 6 oz (185 mL) milk
- ☐ ¹/₄ cup (¹/₂ stick/60 g) butter
- ☐ 3 tablespoons all-purpose flour
- ☐ 3 eggs, separated
- ☐ 6 oz (185 g) canned pumpkin
- ☐ 1 teaspoon grated orange rind
- ☐ 1 teaspoon Pumpkin Pie spice
- ☐ ¹/₂ cup (100 g) finely chopped pitted prunes
- ☐ 2 tablespoons orange juice
- ☐ 1 tablespoon Cointreau (optional)
- ☐ 2 egg whites
- ☐ 3 tablespoons superfine sugar

1   Place sugar, vanilla and milk in a saucepan. Cook over a medium heat, stirring constantly without boiling, until sugar dissolves. Set aside to cool slightly.

2   Melt butter in a saucepan, remove from heat and stir in flour. Cook over medium heat for 2 minutes. Gradually blend in milk mixture and cook over medium heat, stirring constantly, until mixture boils and thickens. Remove from heat and quickly whisk in egg yolks.

3   Combine pumpkin, orange rind, pie spice, prunes, orange juice and Cointreau and stir into egg yolk mixture. Whisk egg whites until stiff peaks form, then fold into pumpkin mixture. Grease an 8-inch (20 cm) soufflé dish and a piece of waxed paper large enough to wrap around the outside of the soufflé dish and extending 1¹/₄ inch (3 cm) above dish. Sprinkle dish and paper with superfine sugar and secure paper around outside of dish with string.

4   Spoon soufflé mixture into prepared soufflé dish and bake at 350°F (180°C) for 25-30 minutes or until cooked.

---

## WHOLEWHEAT FLAPJACKS WITH HONEY BUTTER

Serves 4

- ☐ ¹/₂ cup (60 g) all-purpose flour
- ☐ ¹/₂ cup (60 g) wholewheat flour
- ☐ 4 tablespoons powdered milk
- ☐ 3 teaspoons baking powder
- ☐ 1 tablespoon packed brown sugar
- ☐ 1 egg, lightly beaten
- ☐ 1 cup (250 mL) water
- ☐ 2 tablespoons (30 g) margarine, melted

HONEY BUTTER
- ☐ ¹/₂ cup (1 stick/125 g) unsalted butter, softened
- ☐ 1¹/₂ tablespoons honey
- ☐ 1 tablespoon IOX (confectioners') sugar
- ☐ 1 teaspoon grated lemon rind

1   Sift together flours, milk powder, baking powder and sugar into a large mixing bowl. Return husks to the bowl. Stir in egg, water and margarine and beat to a smooth batter using a wooden spoon.

2   Drop approximately 2 tablespoons of batter into a heated, lightly greased skillet and cook until bubbly and browned underneath, then turn and cook other side. Remove from pan and set aside to keep warm. Repeat with remaining mixture.

3   To make Honey Butter: Place butter, honey, confectioners' sugar and lemon rind in a bowl and beat until smooth and creamy. Serve with warm flapjacks.

---

## APRICOT PASSIONFRUIT SLICE

Serves 6

- ☐ 1¹/₃ cups (140 g) rolled oats
- ☐ ³/₄ cup (125 g) packed brown sugar
- ☐ 1 cup (125 g) wholewheat flour
- ☐ ¹/₂ teaspoon baking powder
- ☐ ³/₄ cup (185 g) margarine, melted
- ☐ 2 teaspoons grated lemon rind

FILLING
- ☐ 1¹/₄ cups (155 g) dried apricots, chopped
- ☐ ¹/₂ cup (125 mL) water
- ☐ ¹/₄ cup (60 mL) passionfruit pulp
- ☐ 2 tablespoons raw sugar

1   Stir together oats, sugar, flour and baking powder in a large bowl. Add margarine and lemon rind, mix well. Press half the mixture over the bottom of a greased 7 x 11-inch (18 x 28 cm) shallow cake pan.

2   To make filling: Combine apricots, water, passionfruit pulp and sugar in a saucepan. Bring to the boil, then reduce heat and simmer until apricots are soft and all liquid is absorbed. Set aside for 5 minutes to cool slightly. Spread evenly over oat layer.

3   Sprinkle remaining oat mixture over filling. Bake at 350°F (180°C) for 45 minutes, or until browned and crisp. Cut into bars and serve warm with cream or yogurt.

*Tiles Pazotti Plates The Bay Tree*

*Spicy Pumpkin and Prune Soufflé, Apricot Passionfruit Slice, Wholewheat Flapjacks with Honey Butter*

## APPLE WAFER STACKS WITH PECAN SAUCE

Serves 4

- ☐ **1 egg white**
- ☐ **3 tablespoons superfine sugar**
- ☐ **$^1/_2$ teaspoon vanilla extract**
- ☐ **2 tablespoons (30 g) butter, melted**
- ☐ **$^1/_4$ cup (30 g) ground hazelnuts**
- ☐ **3 tablespoons all-purpose flour, sifted**
- ☐ **3 tablespoons IOX (confectioners') sugar**

APPLE FILLING
- ☐ **2 large green apples, cored, peeled and thinly sliced**
- ☐ **2 tablespoons honey**
- ☐ **4 tablespoons water**
- ☐ **2 tablespoons golden raisins**
- ☐ **1 teaspoon grated lemon rind**

PECAN SAUCE
- ☐ **$^1/_2$ cup (125 g) superfine sugar**
- ☐ **3 tablespoons water**
- ☐ **$^1/_2$ cup (125 mL) light cream**
- ☐ **3 tablespoons (45 g) margarine**
- ☐ **3 tablespoons chopped pecans**

1   Place egg white in a mixing bowl and whisk until soft peaks form. Gradually add sugar, beating well after each addition.

Fold in vanilla, butter, nuts and flour.
2   Place heaped teaspoons of mixture on lightly greased cookie sheets, about 4 inches (10 cm) apart. Spread mixture out to about 2 inches (5 cm) in diameter, using the back of a spoon. Bake at 350°F (180°C) for 5 minutes or until edges are golden. Cool on sheets for 2-3 minutes before lifting on to wire racks to cool completely. Repeat with remaining mixture to make sixteen wafers.
3   To make filling: Place apples, honey and water in a saucepan. Bring to the boil, then reduce heat and simmer covered for 10-15 minutes, or until apples are soft. Stir in raisins and lemon rind. Set aside.
4   To make sauce: Place sugar and water in a saucepan. Cook over medium heat, stirring constantly, without boiling, until sugar dissolves. Then bring to the boil and boil without stirring until mixture is a light golden color. Remove pan from heat and carefully stir in cream. Cook over medium heat, stirring constantly, until mixture is smooth. Stir in margarine and nuts.
5   Place one wafer on four serving plates, spread each with apple filling. Top with next wafer. Repeat with remaining filling and wafers, making a stack of four wafers, finishing with a wafer. Dust with confectioners' sugar, spoon over sauce and serve immediately.

*Apple Wafer Stacks with Pecan Sauce*

Glass The Bay Tree

## STRAWBERRY AND RHUBARB SOUFFLES

*Light, sweet and tangy, these individual soufflés will complement a rich main meal. Sprinkled with confectioners' sugar and served with fresh strawberries and whipped cream, who could possibly resist them?*

Serves 4

- ☐ **5 oz (155 g) strawberries, halved**
- ☐ **5 oz (155 g) chopped fresh rhubarb**
- ☐ **²/₃ cup (155 g) superfine sugar**
- ☐ **2 tablespoons lemon juice**
- ☐ **3 teaspoons gelatin dissolved in 2 tablespoons hot water**
- ☐ **2 egg whites**
- ☐ **1 cup (250 mL) heavy cream, lightly whipped**

1   Place strawberries, rhubarb, sugar and lemon juice in a saucepan and cook over medium heat, stirring until sugar dissolves. Bring to the boil, then reduce heat and simmer, covered, for 15 minutes or until rhubarb is tender. Remove from heat. Press mixture through a sieve into a bowl and stir in gelatin mixture. Set aside to cool.

2   Whisk egg whites until stiff peaks form and fold into strawberry mixture. Fold in cream and spoon mixture into six individual soufflé dishes with 1¹/₄-inch (3 cm) high aluminum foil collars attached. Refrigerate until firm. Remove foil collars and serve.

## RASPBERRY PASSION-FRUIT SORBET

*A refreshingly icy dessert that is most suitable to follow a curry, satay or other spicy dish. Fresh, frozen or drained canned raspberries can be used for the purée in this recipe.*

Serves

- ☐ **2 cups (500 mL) water**
- ☐ **¹/₂ cup (125 g) sugar**
- ☐ **¹/₄ cup (60 mL) sieved passionfruit juice**
- ☐ **¹/₂ cup (125 mL) sieved raspberry purée**
- ☐ **1 egg white**

1   Combine water and sugar in a saucepan and cook over low heat, stirring constantly, until sugar dissolves. Bring to the boil, reduce heat and simmer for 2 minutes. Remove from heat and set aside to cool.

2   Stir passionfruit juice and raspberry purée into syrup. Pour into a freezer tray and freeze until firm.

3   Chop mixture roughly and place in a food processor or blender with egg white and process until smooth. Return mixture to freezer tray and freeze until firm.

### COOK'S TIP

The sorbet can be beaten using an electric mixer rather than a food processor. Just beat the mixture until it is smooth.

*Strawberry and Rhubarb Soufflés, Almond Cherry Gâteau (page 76), Raspberry Passionfruit Sorbet*

Carob Hazelnut Macaroons, Rose Water Rice Pudding

Serving Dish The Bay Tree Cane Tray Mosmania

---

## ❖
## ALMOND CHERRY GATEAU

*Creamy-filled and layered, this gâteau is magnificent for any special occasion.*

Serves 8

- ☐ **3 eggs**
- ☐ **1 teaspoon almond extract**
- ☐ **$^1/_4$ cup (60 g) superfine sugar**
- ☐ **5 tablespoons all-purpose flour sifted with 3 tablespoons corn-starch and $^1/_2$ teaspoon baking powder**
- ☐ **$^1/_2$ cup (60 g) ground almonds**

CHERRY FILLING
- ☐ **$^1/_3$ cup (100 g) cherry preserves**
- ☐ **8 oz (250 g) ricotta cheese**

CREAM TOPPING
- ☐ **3 tablespoons cherry preserves**
- ☐ **6 oz (185 g) cream cheese**
- ☐ **2 tablespoons IOX (confectioners') sugar, sifted**
- ☐ **$^1/_4$ cup (60 mL) light cream**
- ☐ **$^1/_2$ cup (60 g) slivered almonds, toasted**

1   Place eggs, almond extract and sugar in a mixing bowl and beat until very thick and creamy. This will take about 10 minutes. Fold in flour mixture and almonds. Pour batter into a greased and waxed paper-lined 9-inch (23 cm) round cake pan. Bake at 350°F (180°C) for 20-25 minutes, or until cake is golden and springs back when gently touched with fingertips. Carefully turn out onto a wire rack to cool. When cold cut into three even layers.
2   To make filling: Place cherry preserves and ricotta cheese in a food processor or blender and process until smooth.
3   Place one cake layer on serving plate and spread with half the filling. Top with another cake layer and remaining filling. Place remaining cake layer on top and refrigerate for 10 minutes.
4   To make topping: Place cherry preserves, cream cheese and confectioners' sugar in a food processor or blender and process until smooth. Pour in cream and continue to process until smooth and thick. Spread topping over top and side of gâteau. Press sliced almonds around side of gâteau and refrigerate until ready to serve.

---

## ❖
## ROSE WATER RICE PUDDING

Serves 4

- ☐ **4 cups (1 litre) milk**
- ☐ **$^3/_4$ cup (185 g) superfine sugar**
- ☐ **1 cup (185 g) short-grain rice**
- ☐ **2 egg yolks, lightly beaten**
- ☐ **2 tablespoons rose water**
- ☐ **ground cardamom**

1   Combine milk and sugar in a heavy saucepan, bring to the boil and stir in rice. Reduce heat to lowest possible temperature, cover with tight-fitting lid and cook for 1 hour, or until almost all the milk has been absorbed. Stir occasionally during cooking.
2   Stir in egg yolks and rose water and remove from heat. Spoon rice into four individual serving dishes or one large dish and dust with cardamom.

## CAROB HAZELNUT MACAROONS

*Carob and hazelnuts combine to make a deliciously new version of an old favorite.*

Makes 30

- ☐ **2 eggs, separated**
- ☐ **³/4 cup (185 g) superfine sugar**
- ☐ **2 tablespoons carob powder, sifted**
- ☐ **2²/3 cups (250 g) dry grated coconut**
- ☐ **¹/2 cup (60 g) roasted hazelnuts, finely chopped**
- ☐ **3¹/2 oz (100 g) carob, melted**

1  Whisk egg whites until soft peaks form. Add sugar, a spoonful at a time, beating well after each addition, until mixture is of meringue consistency.
2  Beat egg yolks with carob powder and lightly fold into egg white mixture. Stir in coconut and hazelnuts. Drop tablespoons of mixture onto greased cookie sheets and bake at 350°F (180°C) for 15 minutes or until firm. Cool on cookie sheets. Drizzle with melted carob.

*Peach Gelatin with Coconut Frâiche*

## PEACH GELATIN WITH COCONUT FRAICHE

*This light dessert with a tangy fruit flavor is guaranteed to tempt all!*

Serves 6

- ☐ **1 cup (250 mL) water**
- ☐ **¹/2 cup (125 g) sugar**
- ☐ **2 tablespoons gelatin dissolved in ¹/2 cup (125 mL) hot water**
- ☐ **1 cup (250 mL) peach nectar**
- ☐ **5 oz (155 mL) strained fresh orange juice**
- ☐ **¹/2 cup (125 mL) canned pineapple juice**

COCONUT FRAICHE
- ☐ **1 cup (250 mL) heavy cream**
- ☐ **3 tablespoons coconut cream**
- ☐ **1 tablespoon dry grated coconut**
- ☐ **3 tablespoons buttermilk**

1  Combine water and sugar in a saucepan and stir over medium heat until sugar dissolves. Bring to the boil, then remove from heat and stir in gelatin, peach nectar, orange and pineapple juices.
2  Pour mixture into an oiled decorative 6-cup (1.2 litre) mold, or six individual molds and refrigerate until firm.
3  To make Coconut Frâiche: combine cream, coconut cream, coconut and buttermilk in a bowl and whisk until smooth. Cover and set aside to stand at room temperature for 24 hours or until mixture is thick. When frâiche has thickened, cover and refrigerate until required.
4  To serve: Unmold gelatin and accompany with frâiche.

---

### ROSE WATER

◇  It is believed that rose water – one of the sweetest smelling essences – was originally brought to India by the Moguls. It became a fashionable flavoring in England during the 16th century and remained a staple ingredient until Victorian times.

◇  One of the first uses for rose water in the Western world was to scent the finger bowls of the wealthy.

◇  As the name implies, rose water is extracted from roses.

◇  Rose water and orange flower water are essential ingredients in Indian and Middle Eastern cooking, where they are used in both savory and sweet dishes.

*These recipes are like the icing on the cake.*
*They provide the little extras that make the difference*
*between a good meal and a memorable one.*

# GOOD
## *companions*

❖

## EGGPLANT CHATNI RELISH

*Spread on toast, add shredded cheese and broil. Store in a screwtop jar in the refrigerator.*

Makes 4 x 8 oz (250 mL) jars

- ☐ **2 large eggplants, cut into thick strips**
- ☐ **salt**
- ☐ **3 tablespoons vegetable oil**
- ☐ **6 green onions, finely chopped**
- ☐ **3 cloves garlic, crushed**
- ☐ **4 small red chilies, seeded and finely chopped**
- ☐ **1 tablespoon finely chopped fresh ginger**
- ☐ **1 teaspoon black mustard seeds**
- ☐ **1 teaspoon ground cumin**
- ☐ **1$^1$/$_4$ cups (315 mL) red wine vinegar**
- ☐ **$^3$/$_4$ cup (125 g) packed brown sugar**
- ☐ **1 teaspoon garam masala**

1  Sprinkle eggplant with salt and set aside for 30 minutes. Rinse under cold running water and pat dry with paper towels.
2    Heat 1 tablespoon oil in a saucepan and cook green onions, garlic, chilies, ginger, mustard seeds and cumin for 2-3 minutes. Remove from pan and set aside. Add remaining oil to pan and cook eggplant for 3-5 minutes, or until browned. Remove from pan.
3   Pour vinegar into pan and heat until almost boiling. Return green onion mixture and eggplant to the pan, reduce heat and cook for 2-3 minutes, stirring gently.
4   Stir in sugar and garam masala. Cook 40-45 minutes longer, or until relish thickens. Pour into hot sterilized jars and seal when cold.

❖❖

## INDIAN PUNJAB SAMBAL

*Eat this spicy vegetable relish immediately or store in the refrigerator for a few days.*

Makes 4 x 8 oz (250 mL) jars

- ☐ **2 red peppers, seeded and chopped**
- ☐ **2 stalks celery, chopped**
- ☐ **2 carrots, peeled and chopped**
- ☐ **2 small zucchini, chopped**
- ☐ **2 green chilies, seeded and finely chopped**
- ☐ **4 large tomatoes, peeled, seeded and chopped**
- ☐ **2 tablespoons vegetable oil**
- ☐ **1 teaspoon cumin seeds**
- ☐ **1 teaspoon yellow mustard seeds**
- ☐ **3 curry leaves, crumbled**
- ☐ **1 small eggplant, cut into small chunks**
- ☐ **1$^1$/$_4$ cups (300 mL) vegetable stock or broth**
- ☐ **1 tablespoon finely chopped cilantro (fresh coriander) leaves**
- ☐ **1 tablespoon finely chopped fresh parsley**

1   Place peppers, celery, carrots, zucchini and chilies in a food processor or blender and process until coarsely chopped. Transfer to a bowl and stir in tomatoes.
2   Heat oil in a saucepan and cook cumin, mustard seeds and curry leaves over high heat for 2-3 minutes. Reduce heat, stir in eggplant and cook for 2 minutes, stirring occasionally.
3   Add vegetable mixture, stock or broth, cilantro and parsley. Bring to the boil, reduce heat and simmer for 25-30 minutes, or until liquid has evaporated and vegetables are tender.

Glassware Villeroy & Boch

## FIG AND WALNUT CHUTNEY

*A splendid accompaniment for your next cheese platter.*

Makes 7 x 8 oz (250 mL) jars

- [ ] 1¹/2 **pounds (750 g) dried figs, cut into quarters**
- [ ] **2 large onions, sliced**
- [ ] 1³/4 **cups (185 g) walnuts, roughly chopped**
- [ ] ¹/2 **cup (90 g) dried dates, pitted and roughly chopped**
- [ ] ¹/2 **cup (90 g) golden raisins**
- [ ] ¹/3 **cup (60 g) preserved ginger in heavy syrup**
- [ ] ¹/2 **teaspoon yellow mustard seeds**
- [ ] ¹/2 **teaspoon ground cinnamon**
- [ ] 1¹/2 **cups (250 g) packed brown sugar**
- [ ] **3 cups (750 mL) cider vinegar**

1 Combine figs, onions, walnuts, dates, raisins, ginger, mustard seeds, cinnamon, sugar and vinegar in a large saucepan. Cook over low heat for 10 minutes, or until sugar dissolves, stirring frequently.

2 Bring to the boil, then reduce heat and simmer uncovered for 1¹/2-2 hours, or until chutney is dark and thick. Pour into hot sterilized jars and seal when cold.

## MANGO CHILI SALSA

*If fresh mangoes are not available, frozen or canned mangoes can be used instead.*

Serves 4

- [ ] **2 large mangoes, peeled, pitted and chopped**
- [ ] **2 green onions, chopped**
- [ ] **1 small red chili, seeded and finely chopped**
- [ ] **1 tablespoon finely chopped cilantro (fresh coriander) leaves**
- [ ] **2 tablespoons fresh orange juice**
- [ ] **freshly ground black pepper**

Place mangoes, green onions, chili, cilantro and orange juice in a bowl and toss to combine. Season to taste with pepper and set aside to stand for 1 hour before serving.

*Clockwise from top left: Cilantro Pesto (page 81), Fig and Walnut Chutney, Mango Chili Salsa, Eggplant Chatni Relish, Indian Punjab Sambal, Lime and Cilantro Chutney (page 81)*

## LIME AND CILANTRO CHUTNEY

Makes 3 x 8 oz (250 mL) jars

- [ ] **10 limes, thinly sliced**
- [ ] **4 large pears, peeled, cored and cut into chunks**
- [ ] **2 cloves garlic, finely chopped**
- [ ] **2¼ cups (375 g) packed brown sugar**
- [ ] **4 tablespoons finely chopped fresh cilantro (coriander) leaves**
- [ ] **¾ cup (185 mL) cider vinegar**
- [ ] **¾ cup (185 mL) water**
- [ ] **1 teaspoon Apple Pie spice**
- [ ] **½ teaspoon finely chopped preserved ginger in heavy syrup**

1  Place limes, pears, garlic, sugar, cilantro, vinegar, water, apple pie spice, and ginger in a large saucepan.
2  Cook over low heat, stirring, until sugar dissolves. Bring to the boil, then reduce heat and simmer, stirring frequently, for 1½ hours or until thick. Pour into hot sterilized jars and seal when cold.

## DRIED APRICOT AND ALMOND CHUTNEY

*A sweet, spicy chutney with a nutty crunch!*

Makes 5 x 8 oz (250 mL) jars

- [ ] **1½ pounds (750 g) dried apricots**
- [ ] **4 cups (1 litre) hot water**
- [ ] **8 cloves garlic, finely chopped**
- [ ] **1¼ cups (315 g) sugar**
- [ ] **¾ cup (125 g) golden raisins**
- [ ] **1 tablespoon finely chopped fresh ginger**
- [ ] **¼ teaspoon ground cayenne pepper**
- [ ] **1¼ cups (300 mL) cider vinegar**
- [ ] **1 cup (125 g) slivered almonds**

1  Place apricots in a bowl, pour over water and set aside to soak for 4 hours.
2  Place apricots and water, garlic, sugar, raisins, ginger, cayenne and vinegar in a large saucepan. Stir over medium heat until sugar dissolves. Bring to the boil, reduce heat and simmer, stirring occasionally, for 45 minutes. Stir in almonds and cook for 45 minutes longer or until chutney thickens. Pour into hot sterilized jars and seal when cold.

*Cutlery Made Where China Pillivuyt*

*Italian Green Sauce with Basil, Mexican Chili Sauce, Spicy Peanut Satay Sauce, Creamy Mustard Sauce*

## CILANTRO PESTO

*A delicious sauce for pasta, an excellent addition to soup, or just serve it as a dip. It will keep for 2-3 days in the refrigerator.*

Makes about 1 cup (250 mL)

- [ ] **3 large bunches cilantro (fresh coriander) leaves**
- [ ] **2 cloves garlic, crushed**
- [ ] **⅓ cup (60 g) pine nuts**
- [ ] **½ cup (125 mL) olive oil**
- [ ] **½ cup (60 g) grated Parmesan cheese**

Place cilantro, garlic and pine nuts in a food processor or blender and process until finely chopped. With machine running, slowly pour in the oil and process until smooth. Add cheese, process to blend.

## ITALIAN GREEN SAUCE WITH BASIL

*Wonderful with hot pasta!*

Makes 1 cup (250 mL)

- [ ] **2 small bunches fresh basil leaves, finely chopped**
- [ ] **3 green onions, finely chopped**
- [ ] **2 cloves garlic, crushed**
- [ ] **1 tablespoon capers, drained and rinsed**
- [ ] **5 oz (155 mL) olive oil**
- [ ] **1 tablespoon lemon juice**
- [ ] **freshly ground black pepper**

Place basil, green onions, garlic and capers in a food processor or blender and process until smooth. With machine running, slowly pour in oil, then lemon juice, and continue to process until well blended. Season to taste with pepper.

## SPICY PEANUT SATAY SAUCE

Makes 1½ cups (375 mL )

- [ ] **2 tablespoons peanut oil**
- [ ] **2 cups (315 g) roasted peanuts, finely chopped**
- [ ] **2 cloves garlic, crushed**
- [ ] **1 onion, finely chopped**
- [ ] **½ teaspoon chili powder**
- [ ] **1 tablespoon packed brown sugar**
- [ ] **2 tablespoons soy sauce**
- [ ] **¼ teaspoon Chinese five spice**
- [ ] **2 cups (500 mL) coconut milk**

1  Heat oil in a saucepan and cook peanuts, garlic, onion and chili powder, stirring for 3-4 minutes.
2  Add sugar, soy sauce and five spice powder, reduce heat and pour in coconut milk. Simmer for 5-10 minutes, stirring occasionally. If sauce becomes too thick, thin with a little whole milk.

## CREAMY MUSTARD SAUCE

*Best made just before serving, this superbly tangy sauce is great poured over steamed vegetables.*

Makes about 1 cup (250 mL)

- [ ] **1¼ cups (315 mL) light cream**
- [ ] **1½ tablespoons coarse grain mustard**
- [ ] **1 clove garlic, crushed**
- [ ] **3 tablespoons vegetable stock or broth**
- [ ] **1 tablespoon finely snipped fresh chives or finely chopped parsley**
- [ ] **freshly ground black pepper**

Place cream in a small saucepan and bring to the boil. Boil rapidly until reduced by a quarter. Stir in mustard, garlic and vegetable stock or broth. Simmer for 5-10 minutes, stirring frequently, until sauce reduces and thickens a little. Stir in chives or parsley and season to taste with pepper.

## MEXICAN CHILI SAUCE

Makes about 2 cups (500 mL)

- [ ] **2 tablespoons sesame oil**
- [ ] **3 small red chilies, seeded and finely chopped**
- [ ] **3 small green chilies, seeded and finely chopped**
- [ ] **3 cloves garlic, crushed**
- [ ] **2 onions, finely chopped**
- [ ] **1 tablespoon finely chopped cilantro (fresh coriander) leaves**
- [ ] **14 oz (440 g) canned peeled tomatoes, undrained and mashed**
- [ ] **1 teaspoon brown sugar**
- [ ] **½ teaspoon ground cinnamon**
- [ ] **¼ teaspoon ground cloves**
- [ ] **¼ teaspoon ground ginger**
- [ ] **2 tablespoons lemon juice**
- [ ] **3 tablespoons water**

Heat oil in a skillet and cook red and green chilies, garlic, onions and cilantro for 2-3 minutes. Stir in tomatoes, sugar, cinnamon, cloves, ginger, lemon juice and water and simmer for 10-15 minutes or until sauce reduces and thickens.

*Learn how to make these basics, and your vegetarian repertoire will be virtually limitless! Your culinary imagination and these recipes can be a dynamic combination.*

# BASIC
## *recipes*

---

## PIZZA FACTS

✧ Pizzas do not have to be round – some are oval, some are rectangular and some have a deep crust and sides, resembling a pie.

✧ You can make this pizza recipe several days in advance. Let it rise, punch it down, cover with plastic food wrap and refrigerate until required. Bring the dough to room temperature 2-3 hours before shaping and allow it to rise a second time.

✧ Pizzas can be made using all-purpose or wholewheat flour or a mixture of both.

There are two types of yeast that are commonly used in pizza making – fresh and dried.

Dried yeast works just as well as fresh, but takes longer to activate. As it is twice as concentrated as fresh yeast, only half the amount is required. 1 tablespoon (15 g) dried yeast has the same raising power as 1 oz (30 g) fresh yeast.

Fresh yeast will keep in a loosely tied polythene bag in the refrigerator for about a week.

Dried yeast will keep in a cool dark place for about six months. Yeast will deteriorate if exposed to air.

Yeast works best in warm conditions. Cold and drafts slow down its growth, whereas an intense heat will kill it.

The amount of yeast required depends on the richness of the dough.

Fresh yeast works best when mixed with liquid that is at about 78°F (25°C) and dried yeast at 104°F (40°C).

An easy way of making sure that the liquid is the right temperature is to bring one-third of it to the boil and add the rest cold.

## ❖
## BASIC PIZZA DOUGH

Makes a 15-16-inch (38-40 cm) pizza

- ☐ 1³/₄ teaspoons active dry yeast or ¹/₂ oz (15 g) fresh yeast, crumbled
- ☐ 11 oz (345 mL) warm water
- ☐ pinch sugar
- ☐ ¹/₂ cup (125 mL) olive oil
- ☐ 4 cups (500 g) all-purpose flour, sifted
- ☐ 1¹/₄ teaspoons salt

1   Place yeast, water and sugar in a large mixing bowl and stir to dissolve the sugar. Set aside for 5 minutes or until mixture begins to foam. Stir in the oil, flour and salt. Mix to form a firm dough.
2   Turn out onto a lightly floured surface and knead well until dough is soft and shiny – this will take about 5 minutes. Place dough in a lightly oiled, large bowl. Roll the dough around in the bowl to coat the surface with oil. Cover with plastic food wrap and set aside in a warm, draft-free place for 1¹/₂-2 hours or until dough has doubled in volume.
3   Remove dough from bowl and punch down. Knead briefly before rolling out on a floured surface to desired shape. If dough feels too stiff, rest it for a few minutes and start again. Lift dough with rolling pin onto an oiled pizza tray. Finish shaping by hand, forming a slightly raised rim about ¹/₄ inch (5 mm) in thickness. Top dough with your favourite topping and bake. If a thicker crust is required, cover base with a towel and set aside for 30 minutes or until it has risen sufficiently.

## ❖
## FOCACCIA DOUGH

*Focaccia is a large flat oval or rectangle of bread from Italy. In its simplest form it is flavored with just olive oil, salt and sometimes, garlic or herbs.*

Makes 1 large focaccia

- ☐ 1 teaspoon active dry yeast, or ¹/₄ oz (8 g) fresh yeast, crumbled
- ☐ 2 tablespoons (30 mL) warm water
- ☐ 1¹/₄ cups (300 mL) water at room temperature
- ☐ 1 tablespoon olive oil
- ☐ 4 cups (500 g) all-purpose flour
- ☐ 2 teaspoons salt

1   Place yeast and warm water in a large bowl and stir to combine. Set aside for 8-10 minutes or until it is foaming. Stir in all but 1 tablespoon of additional water and the oil.
2   Add one-third of the flour and the salt and stir until smooth. Stir in another third of flour and beat well. Add remaining flour and mix until a rough dough forms. Turn out onto a floured surface and knead well for 8-10 minutes or until smooth and shiny.
3   Place dough in a large, lightly oiled bowl, and roll dough around in bowl to coat the surface with oil. Seal with plastic food wrap and set aside in a warm, draft-free position for 1¹/₂ hours or until doubled in volume.
4   Punch down dough, knead once or twice and roll to desired shape. Place on an oiled tray, cover with a towel and set aside in the same warm spot for 30 minutes longer.
5   Dimple the entire surface of the dough with fingertips, pushing down about half-way. Re-cover with the towel and set aside for 1¹/₂-2 hours or until doubled in size. Focaccia is now ready for topping and baking.

## EGGPLANT, GORGONZOLA AND SAGE TOPPING

*Try this delicious topping on pizza or focaccia.*

- [ ] **1 large eggplant, 2-2$\frac{1}{2}$ inches (5-6 cm) in diameter, cut into $\frac{1}{4}$-inch (5 mm) slices**
- [ ] **salt**
- [ ] **$\frac{3}{4}$ cup (185 mL) olive oil**
- [ ] **5 oz (155 g) Gorgonzola or blue cheese, mashed**
- [ ] **12 oz (375 g) ricotta cheese, drained**
- [ ] **1 teaspoon finely chopped fresh sage, or $\frac{1}{4}$ teaspoon dried sage**
- [ ] **3 tablespoons pine nuts**
- [ ] **3 tablespoons grated Parmesan cheese**
- [ ] **freshly ground black pepper**
- [ ] **3 sage leaves**

1   Place eggplant in a colander, sprinkle with salt and set aside to drain for about 30 minutes. Rinse under cold running water and pat dry on paper towels.

2   Heat $\frac{1}{2}$ cup (125 mL) olive oil in a large skillet and cook eggplant slices, a few at a time, until lightly golden on each side. Remove from pan and drain on paper towels.

3   Brush prepared pizza dough with one tablespoon olive oil. Combine Gorgonzola and ricotta cheeses and spread evenly over base within the rim. Arrange eggplant slices over top. Sprinkle with sage, pine nuts, Parmesan cheese and black pepper to taste. Drizzle over remaining oil and decorate with sage leaves. Bake at 425°F (220°C) for 15 minutes. Reduce temperature to 375°F (190°C) and bake for 10 minutes longer, or until crust is golden and the Parmesan and pine nuts are browned.

## VEGETABLE STOCK

*The best vegetable stock ever and well worth the effort to make. It will add a delicious flavor to any dish, and is a must for any vegetarian cook.*

Makes 8 cups (2 litres)

- [ ] **2 large onions, quartered**
- [ ] **2 large carrots, peeled and roughly chopped**
- [ ] **1 head celery, leaves included, roughly chopped**
- [ ] **1 bunch parsley, stalks included**
- [ ] **$\frac{1}{2}$ teaspoon whole black peppercorns**
- [ ] **10 cups (2.5 litres) cold water**

1   Place onions, carrots, celery, parsley, peppercorns and water in a large stockpot. Bring to the boil, reduce heat and simmer for 30 minutes, stirring occasionally.

2   Remove from heat and allow to cool. Purée cold vegetable mixture, then push through a sieve. Use as required.

### WATCHPOINT

Do not add salt when making stock, especially if you do not know how it is to be used. Salting stock can lead to an over-salty dish if you reduce the stock or if you are using other salty ingredients.

### THE FLAVOR BOOSTER

✧   You don't have to be a gourmet to realize that many good dishes rely on stock for a rich flavor.

✧   The essential ingredients to make a wholesome vegetable stock are onions, carrots, celery and some herbs – fresh if possible.

✧   The ingredients should be roughly chopped to extract as much flavor as possible during cooking.

✧   The longer the stock cooks, the more concentrated the flavor.

**Vegetables:** Carrots, onions, celery and leeks are the most popular stock vegetables.

✧   Vegetables such as turnip, cauliflower and leafy green vegetables tend to have too strong a flavor to use in stock. However, parsnips and overripe tomatoes are an excellent addition to the stockpot.

**Herbs and spices:** Bay leaves, thyme and parsley are the most popular stock herbs. Include parsley stalks as well as the leaves.

✧   Use peppercorns but not salt, for seasoning.

## TOFU MAYONNAISE

*This delicious mayonnaise made with tofu is a low-fat, no-egg alternative to traditional mayonnaise. Try it with rice or potato salads.*

Makes 1$^{1}/_{2}$ cups (375 mL)

- [ ] 8 oz (250 g) tofu
- [ ] 1 teaspoon Dijon-style mustard
- [ ] 3 tablespoons cider vinegar
- [ ] $^{1}/_{2}$ cup (125 mL) olive oil
- [ ] freshly ground black pepper

1   Place tofu, mustard and 1 tablespoon vinegar in a food processor or blender and process until smooth.
2   With the machine running, slowly add 2 tablespoons oil then another tablespoon vinegar. Continue in this way until all the oil and vinegar are used. Season to taste with pepper.

## GINGER AND SOY DRESSING

Makes 1 cup (250 mL)

- [ ] 1 tablespoon sesame oil
- [ ] 1 tablespoon grated fresh ginger
- [ ] $^{1}/_{2}$ cup (125 mL) salt-reduced soy sauce
- [ ] $^{1}/_{2}$ cup (125 mL) water
- [ ] 1 tablespoon cider vinegar
- [ ] 1 clove garlic, crushed

Combine sesame oil, ginger, soy sauce, water, vinegar and garlic in a screw-top jar. Shake well to combine. Stand 15 minutes before using.

## ORIENTAL MAYONNAISE

Makes 1$^{1}/_{2}$ cups (375 mL)

- [ ] 1 clove garlic, crushed
- [ ] 2 teaspoons grated fresh ginger
- [ ] 4 tablespoons soy sauce
- [ ] 2 tablespoons cider vinegar
- [ ] 2 tablespoons packed brown sugar
- [ ] 1 teaspoon fennel seeds
- [ ] 2 egg yolks
- [ ] $^{1}/_{2}$ teaspoon dry mustard
- [ ] $^{3}/_{4}$ cup (185 mL) vegetable oil
- [ ] 2 teaspoons sesame oil
- [ ] $^{1}/_{2}$ teaspoon hot chili sauce

1   Place garlic, ginger, soy sauce, vinegar, sugar and fennel seeds in a small saucepan and bring to the boil. Reduce heat and simmer, uncovered, for 10 minutes or until mixture reduces by half. Remove from heat and strain to remove fennel seeds. Set aside to cool.
2   Place egg yolks and dry mustard in a food processor or blender. Process until just combined. With machine running, pour in vegetable and sesame oils in a steady stream. Process until mayonnaise thickens.
3   Add soy mixture and process to combine. Mix in the chili sauce to taste.

## PROCESSOR MAYONNAISE

Makes 1$^{1}/_{2}$ cups (375 mL)

- [ ] 2 egg yolks
- [ ] $^{1}/_{4}$ teaspoon dry mustard
- [ ] 1 cup (250 mL) olive oil
- [ ] 2 tablespoons white wine vinegar
- [ ] freshly ground black pepper

Place egg yolks and mustard in a food processor. With machine running, slowly pour in olive oil and process until mixture thickens. Blend in vinegar and season to taste with pepper.

## SWEET CURRY MAYONNAISE

*Serve as a dressing for salads or as a dipping sauce for vegetables.*

Makes $^{1}/_{2}$ cup (125 mL)

- [ ] $^{1}/_{2}$ cup (125 mL) mayonnaise
- [ ] 2 teaspoons curry powder
- [ ] 2 teaspoons apricot jam
- [ ] pinch ground turmeric
- [ ] 2 tablespoons light cream

Place mayonnaise, curry powder, apricot jam, turmeric and cream in a bowl. Mix well to combine.

## VINAIGRETTE

*A salad made from salad greens is not a salad without a tangy coating of vinaigrette to tantalize the taste buds.*

- [ ] $^{3}/_{4}$ cup (185 mL) olive oil
- [ ] 3 tablespoons cider vinegar
- [ ] 1 tablespoon Dijon-style mustard
- [ ] freshly ground black pepper

Place oil, vinegar and mustard in a screw-top jar. Season to taste with pepper. Shake well to combine.

*Variations*

**Walnut or Hazelnut Dressing:** Replace olive oil with 4 tablespoons walnut or hazelnut oil and 1$^{1}/_{4}$ cups (315 mL) vegetable oil.

**Lemon and Herb Vinaigrette:** Replace vinegar with 3 tablespoons lemon juice, add $^{1}/_{4}$ cup (60 g) mixed chopped fresh herbs, such as basil, parsley, chives, rosemary, thyme or tarragon.

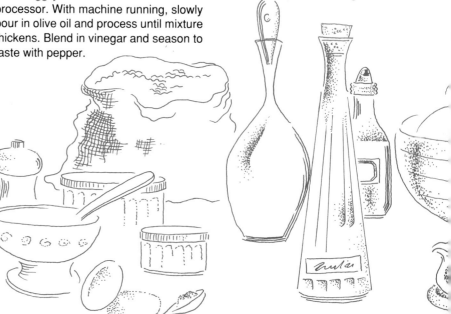

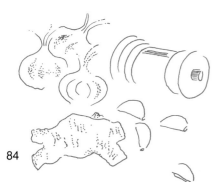

## BASIC WHITE SAUCE

Makes 1 cup (250 mL)

- ☐ **2 tablespoons (30 g) butter**
- ☐ **2 tablespoons all-purpose flour**
- ☐ **$1/4$ teaspoon dry mustard**
- ☐ **1 cup (250 mL) milk**

1   Melt butter in a saucepan, stir in flour and mustard and cook over medium heat for 1 minute.
2   Remove pan from heat and whisk in milk a little at a time until well blended. Cook over medium heat, stirring constantly, until sauce boils and thickens.

*Variations*

**Cheese Sauce:** When sauce thickens, remove from heat and stir in $1/2$ cup (60 g) shredded Cheddar cheese. Serve immediately, and avoid reheating as cheese becomes tough and stringy if stirred over direct heat.
**Mushroom Sauce:** Cook $3 1/2$ oz (100 g) button mushrooms in butter. Remove from pan and set aside. Continue cooking as for Basic White Sauce, replacing 3 tablespoons of milk with cream. When sauce thickens, return mushrooms to the pan and heat through.
**Curry Sauce:** Cook 2 teaspoons curry powder and 1 small finely chopped onion in butter. Cook for 2-3 minutes before adding flour, then continue as for Basic White Sauce.

## ONION AND HERB YOGURT SAUCE

*Try this low-calorie (kilojoule) sauce as an alternative to white sauce. Serve as an accompaniment to vegetables or vegetarian dishes.*

Makes $1 1/4$ cups (315 mL)

- ☐ **1 tablespoon olive oil**
- ☐ **1 onion, finely chopped**
- ☐ **$1/4$ teaspoon ground coriander**
- ☐ **2 tablespoons all-purpose flour**
- ☐ **$1/2$ cup (125 mL) low-fat milk**
- ☐ **6 oz (185 g) plain low-fat yogurt**
- ☐ **1 tablespoon finely chopped fresh basil**
- ☐ **1 tablespoon finely chopped fresh parsley**
- ☐ **1 tablespoon finely snipped fresh chives**
- ☐ **freshly ground black pepper**

1   Heat oil in a saucepan and cook onion and coriander for 4-5 minutes or until onion softens. Stir in flour and gradually mix in milk. Reduce heat and cook until sauce thickens.
2   Mix in yogurt, basil, parsley and chives and stir over low heat until heated through. Season to taste with pepper.

## RICH TOMATO SAUCE

Makes $1 1/2$ cups (375 mL)

- ☐ **1 tablespoon olive oil**
- ☐ **1 onion, sliced**
- ☐ **1 clove garlic, crushed**
- ☐ **$1/2$ green pepper, sliced**
- ☐ **14 oz (440 g) canned tomatoes, undrained and chopped**
- ☐ **$1/2$ cup (125 mL) dry white wine**
- ☐ **1 teaspoon dried mixed herbs**
- ☐ **freshly ground black pepper**

1   Heat oil in a saucepan and cook onion, garlic and green pepper for 4-5 minutes until onion softens. Stir in tomatoes and wine and simmer for 5 minutes.
2   Add herbs and season to taste with black pepper. Simmer for 20 minutes longer or until sauce reduces and thickens.

## LIME AND LEMON SAUCE

Makes 2 cups (500 mL)

- ☐ **$1/4$ cup ($1/2$ stick/60 g) butter**
- ☐ **1 clove garlic, crushed**
- ☐ **$1 1/2$ tablespoons cornstarch blended with 3 tablespoons water**
- ☐ **2 cups (500 mL) vegetable stock or broth**
- ☐ **1 tablespoon lemon juice**
- ☐ **1 tablespoon lime juice**
- ☐ **$1/2$ teaspoon grated lime rind**
- ☐ **$1/2$ teaspoon grated lemon rind**
- ☐ **pinch ground turmeric**

Melt butter in a saucepan and cook garlic for 1 minute. Stir in cornstarch mixture, vegetable stock or broth, lemon and lime juices, lime and lemon rinds and turmeric. Cook over medium heat, stirring constantly until sauce boils and thickens.

## RICH SHORTCRUST PASTRY

*Rich shortcrust pastry can be used for both sweet and savory pies.*

- ☐ **2 cups (250 g) all-purpose flour, sifted**
- ☐ **³/₄ cup(1¹/₂ sticks/185 g) butter, chilled and cut into small cubes**
- ☐ **1 egg yolk, lightly beaten**
- ☐ **3-4 tablespoons water, chilled**

1   Place flour into a medium bowl and rub in butter using your fingertips until mixture resembles bread crumbs.
2   Mix in egg yolk and enough water to form a soft dough with a metal spatula or round-ended knife.
3   Turn onto a lightly floured surface and knead gently until smooth. Cover with plastic food wrap and refrigerate for 30 minutes. Roll out and use as desired.

## ALMOND PASTRY SHELLS

*Bake these pastry shells and serve filled with lemon butter or your favorite jam as an afternoon tea treat.*

- ☐ **3 tablespoons superfine sugar**
- ☐ **vanilla extract**
- ☐ **ingredients for Rich Shortcrust Pastry**
- ☐ **3 tablespoons ground almonds**

1   Add sugar to flour and a few drops of vanilla extract to egg yolk. Continue as directed for shortcrust pastry.
2   Roll out pastry on a lightly floured surface to ¹/₈-inch (3 mm)) thickness. Sprinkle with almonds and cut into 2-inch (5 cm) rounds with a pastry cutter.
3   Line tartlet (patty) pans with pastry rounds, prick bottoms with a fork and bake at 400°F (200°C) for 15-20 minutes or until golden. Remove from tartlet pans and cool on a wire rack.

## CHEESE PASTRY

*Cheese pastry makes a tasty pastry for savory pies. Omit the mustard and pepper and this pastry is perfect with apples or pears.*

- ☐ **³/₄ cup (90 g) shredded Cheddar cheese**
- ☐ **1¹/₂ teaspoons dry mustard**
- ☐ **¹/₂ teaspoon cayenne pepper**
- ☐ **ingredients for Rich Shortcrust Pastry**

Place cheese, mustard, cayenne pepper and flour in a large mixing bowl and continue as directed for shortcrust pastry.

### BAKING BLIND

✧   Baking blind means to precook the pastry shell without a filling. This is done if the filling you are using requires little or no cooking. It is also used when a liquid filling such as a quiche filling is being put into the pastry shell. The precooking then prevents the pastry becoming soggy.
✧   To bake blind, line the pastry shell with baking paper or aluminum foil, then cover the bottom with uncooked rice, pasta or dried beans. This keeps the bottom of the pastry shell flat during cooking. Keep a container on hand to store blind-bake beans or rice, so that they can be used over and over.

*Line pastry shell with paper and weigh down with beans, rice or pasta*

### Tips for perfect pastry making

✧   The best pastry is made using chilled butter and water. It also helps to have utensils cool, so in hot weather it is a good idea to place them in the refrigerator for 10-15 minutes before starting.
✧   Handle the pastry quickly and lightly, as overhandling will result in tough pastry that will be difficult to roll.
✧   The amount of liquid used to bind the ingredients together will vary depending on the quality of the flour. If the dough is too soft the pastry will shrink on cooking.
✧   Kneading the pastry should be done using the coolest part of your hands, the fingertips. After kneading, wrap the pastry in plastic food wrap and refrigerate for 30 minutes before rolling out.
✧   Always roll pastry in light, short strokes, starting from the middle of the pastry, rolling away from you and lifting the rolling pin off the edge of pastry. This ensures even thickness.
✧   Lift and turn the pastry on a floured surface as you roll.
✧   Line the pie plate, trim the edges and rest the pastry in the refrigerator for 10 minutes longer before baking.

### Food processor pastry

✧   The food processor is great for making pastry. Place the flour and butter in the food processor and pulse to cut the butter. Add egg yolk and water and process until dough is just formed. Turn out and knead lightly until smooth. Allow to rest before rolling. You may not require as much water, just sufficient so that the ingredients bind together.

### Filo pastry

✧   Filo (strudel dough) pastry is available from most supermarkets and delicatessens and can be purchased from the freezer or refrigerator sections in your supermarket.
✧   One is equally as good as another. However, once thawed do not refreeze. If you are calorie (kilojoule) conscious, filo pastry is ideal as the fat content is minimal and very little is required when preparing a dish.
✧   When working with this type of pastry, it is important to keep it covered, as the thin sheets have a tendency to dry and break up. Cover sheets not being used immediately with plastic food wrap, then a damp tea-towel.

*Set aside some time each week to plan your family's meals. Drawing up a master grocery list as you go means you will always have all the ingredients you need to create delicious meals. Use the pantry checklist as a handy reminder to make your shopping easier.*

# VEGETARIAN
## *pantry check list*

## STAPLE ITEMS
- [ ] agar agar
- [ ] baking powder
- [ ] baking soda
- [ ] bran
- [ ] bread crumbs, dried
- [ ] brown sugar
- [ ] cocoa powder
- [ ] coffee
- [ ] cream of tartar
- [ ] flour, all-purpose, wholewheat
- [ ] gelatin
- [ ] granulated sugar
- [ ] IOX (confectioners') sugar
- [ ] rolled oats
- [ ] semolina
- [ ] superfine sugar
- [ ] tea
- [ ] yeast

## RICE AND PASTA
- [ ] brown rice
- [ ] white rice, long- and short-grain
- [ ] wild rice
- [ ] wholewheat pasta
- [ ] colored pasta
- [ ] selection pasta shapes
- [ ] instant lasagne sheets
- [ ] Asian noodles

## LEGUMES
(store dried legumes in airtight containers)
- [ ] selection canned beans
- [ ] selection dried beans
- [ ] chickpeas
- [ ] selection legumes

## NUTS, SEEDS, FRUITS
(store nuts and seeds in airtight containers and dried fruit in the refrigerator)
- [ ] almonds
- [ ] peanuts
- [ ] cashew nuts
- [ ] pine nuts
- [ ] sesame seeds
- [ ] sunflower seeds
- [ ] poppy seeds
- [ ] shredded coconut
- [ ] dry grated coconut
- [ ] dried apricots
- [ ] dried figs
- [ ] prunes
- [ ] dried dates
- [ ] raisins

## CANNED FOODS
- [ ] asparagus spears
- [ ] baked beans
- [ ] corn kernels
- [ ] evaporated milk
- [ ] coconut milk or cream
- [ ] selection canned fruits
- [ ] spaghetti
- [ ] tomatoes, whole peeled or puréed
- [ ] tomato paste

## OILS, VINEGARS, SAUCES
- [ ] olive oil
- [ ] sesame oil
- [ ] vinegar, white, cider
- [ ] balsamic vinegar
- [ ] rice vinegar
- [ ] selection herb vinegars
- [ ] soy sauce
- [ ] catsup

## REFRIGERATOR ITEMS
- [ ] eggs
- [ ] yogurt
- [ ] milk
- [ ] selection cheeses
- [ ] margarine
- [ ] mayonnaise
- [ ] olives
- [ ] sun-dried tomatoes
- [ ] tahini

## FREEZER FOODS
- [ ] filo pastry
- [ ] puff pastry
- [ ] selection frozen vegetables

## RELISHES AND SPREADS
- [ ] chutney
- [ ] honey
- [ ] selection jams
- [ ] peanut butter
- [ ] pickles

## HERBS AND SPICES
- [ ] allspice, ground
- [ ] basil leaves, dried
- [ ] black pepper, whole
- [ ] black pepper, ground
- [ ] cayenne pepper
- [ ] chili powder
- [ ] cilantro (fresh coriander) leaves
- [ ] cinnamon, ground
- [ ] coriander, ground
- [ ] cumin, ground
- [ ] curry powder
- [ ] fennel seeds
- [ ] ginger, ground
- [ ] mixed dried herbs
- [ ] mixed spice, ground
- [ ] nutmeg, ground
- [ ] oregano leaves
- [ ] paprika, ground
- [ ] rosemary leaves
- [ ] sage, ground
- [ ] tarragon leaves
- [ ] thyme, dried

## BREADS
- [ ] pita bread
- [ ] wholegrain bread
- [ ] rye bread
- [ ] selection wholegrain rolls
- [ ] wholewheat fruit bread

*You've looked through this book. You've tried – and loved – the recipes. Now, how do you put it all together? This chapter looks at creating a balanced meal and includes tips for successful menu planning.*

# EASY MENU
## *planning*

*Perfect Menu Planning*

**Plan meals:** Set aside some time each week to plan your family's meals for the week ahead. Writing down your menus allows you to quickly see if you are going to serve two very similar meals or dishes close together or use the same ingredients. It is also a good opportunity to check the cooking methods that you are using. Being aware of this when writing your menus will insure that you use a variety of cooking methods, and you can be sure to limit the more unhealthy cooking methods such as frying. Menu planning eliminates those anxious moments of what to feed the family in an hour.

**Shopping lists:** As you plan your week's menus, draw up a master grocery list. Shopping lists insure that you don't forget vital ingredients and that you buy the correct quantities.

**Read recipes:** If you are making a recipe for the first time, read it through in advance, as this will alert you to any special preparation requirements such as soaking beans, making stock or marinating. There is nothing more disappointing than planning to cook a dish, and then realizing an hour before you wish to eat, that it will take you three hours to prepare because the main ingredient requires soaking or marinating first. You will also be advised of any unfamiliar techniques that can slow down the preparation and cooking time. Reading the recipe through and assembling all your ingredients before you start cooking will save you time.

**Using leftovers:** It is economical and practical to use leftovers from one meal in the next. Use leftover vegetable or nutloaf as a sandwich filling with chutney or relish. Leftover vegetables are great to add to soups and baked dishes. Leftover mashed potato can be made into fritters, croquettes or a topping on a pie. Leftover boiled or steamed potatoes make delicious potato salads. Leftover breads, cakes and biscuits made wonderful bread and butter pudding.

**Balanced meals:** The most important function of menu planning is to insure that you are serving a balanced diet. If each meal is nutritionally balanced, it will help to insure that you and your family maintain good health.

*Time Savers*

**Salad preparation:** Save time by storing salad ingredients and some canned products in the refrigerator. Salads can then be served immediately.

**Precook ingredients:** Precious time can be saved by keeping precooked rice, pasta or legumes in the refrigerator or freezer. Always cook extra rice, barley, lentils, beans and chickpeas.

A bowl of cooked rice can be quickly made into:
- Dolmas *(page 18)*
- Rice Fritters *(page 30)*
- An accompaniment for Indian Egg Curry *(page 31)*
- Brown Rice and Vegetable Pie *(page 48)*
- Rice Terrine *(page 56)*
- Indian Sweet Potato Rice Pie *(page 60)*
- Three-Rice Salad Wrapped in Leaves *(page 66)*

Cooked lentils can be made into:
- Lentil Wontons with Cilantro Sauce *(page 18)*
- Spicy Pea Parathas *(page 62)*
- A pâté. Simply purée and flavor with garlic and your favorite spices.
- A vegetable soup, to make a substantial meal.

**Remember to soak:** When legumes are an important part of your diet get into the habit of remembering to soak them the night before.

**Cook ahead:** Cook more than you require then freeze some so that you have prepared meals on hand. If half the family suddenly doesn't turn up for dinner, freeze the leftovers. Freezing in individual portions is great for those times when only one or two are at home for a meal.

**Reduce cooking times:** If you are always short of time, a pressure cooker may be the answer. Cooking time for legumes will be reduced considerably. Canned beans will also save time as these only need reheating.

# DREAMING UP A MENU

*Waste not, want not*

✧ Vegetable and fruit trimmings are often thrown away. With a little thought, many of these can be used in a variety of ways such as adding flavor to other dishes. Try some of the following to make the most of all your food.

✧ Beet greens (leaves and stalks) can be cooked like spinach and served as a vegetable. Alternatively, chop the stalks and use tossed in a salad.

✧ Spinach stalks add a great flavor to stocks and soups. They are also delicious when chopped and stir-fried in butter and garlic and served as a vegetable.

✧ Broccoli stems take a little longer to cook than the heads, but are just as delicious. Chop and serve as a vegetable by themselves, or put on to cook a few minutes before the heads.

✧ Apple cores and fruit skins can be boiled in a saucepan with water, honey and spices, then strained and used as a delicious fruit jelly base. Freeze these trimmings until you have 16 oz (500 g) or more to make this a worthwhile exercise.

✧ Parsley stalks are an essential ingredient in stocks and soups and can be either blended or removed before serving. These can be frozen until required.

✧ Celery leaves are great to use as a garnish or for flavoring. Dry in a cool oven, crumble and store in an airtight container. Use as a flavoring in soups, baked dishes or stews when you do not have fresh celery.

❖

## FAMILY PICNIC FOR SIX

Roasted Red Pepper Quiches
*(page 56)*
Rice Terrine
*(page 56)*
Eggs with Fresh Herb Dressing
*(page 56)*
Marinated Eggplant and Tomato Salad
*(page 61)*
Fresh Fruit

❖

## WINTER DINNER FOR FOUR

Curried Lentil and Vegetable Soup
*(page 19)*
Gingered Vegetables in Bread Baskets
(Make up 1½ recipe quantity)
*(page 16)*
Crusty Bread
Apricot Passionfruit Slice
*(page 72)*

❖

## MAKE A MEAL OF A POTATO

Sweet Potato Soup with Ginger and Lime
*(page 15)*
Potatoes with the Tasty Filling of your choice
*(page 20)*
Watercress and Goat Cheese Salad
*(page 67)*
Lime and Coconut Baked Custard
*(page 69)*

❖

## DINNER IN A HURRY FOR ONE

Blue Cheese and Apple Omelet
*(page 29)*
Wholewheat Roll
Fresh Fruit

❖

## BARBECUE FOR SIX

Vegetable Kebabs with Nutty Avocado Sauce
(Make up 1½ recipe quantity)
*(page 60)*
Herbed Hot Dogs
*(page 58)*
Marinated Mushroom Salad
*(page 58)*
Coleslaw
Crunchy Almond Honey Bars
*(page 52)*

❖

## FAMILY DINNER FOR FOUR

Spinach and Tomato Crêpe Bake
*(page 12)*
(Use this quantity for a main meal for four)
Steamed Vegetables of your choice
Italian Green Sauce with Basil
*(page 81)*
Wholewheat Flapjacks with Honey Butter
*(page 72)*

❖

## SUMMER LUNCH PARTY FOR EIGHT

Savory Avocados with Pistachios
(Make up 1½ recipe quantity)
*(page 14)*
Polenta Croquettes with Tomato Sauce
*(page 24)*
Mixed Lettuce and Fresh Herb Salad
Honey and Carrot Ricotta Roll
*(page 71)*

*The specially developed recipes in this cookbook use many ingredients that may be unfamiliar to newcomers to vegetarian cuisine.*

# VEGETARIAN
## *foods explained*

**A**gar agar. Agar agar is an extract of seaweed and is the vegetarian substitute for gelatin. It comes in either small transparent strips of various colors, or powder form. When dissolved in water over a low heat, agar agar blends with water and on cooling sets to a jelly. It is very important that agar agar is completely dissolved before cooking. Stir into boiling water and simmer over a low heat for 5 minutes. It will set in about an hour at room temperature. To set 8 fl oz (250 mL) of liquid you will require ¼ oz (8 g) agar agar.

**B**uckwheat. Available as roasted or unroasted grains, it is an excellent substitute for rice.

**B**uckwheat flour. Made from buckwheat, it is wonderfully light and can be mixed with wheat flour or used on its own. Best known for its use in Russian blinis.

**C**arob. This cocoa-like powder is the dried, ground seeds of the carob tree. Unlike cocoa powder and chocolate, it is caffeine free. Unfortunately, it is no lower in calories/kilojoules than cocoa powder.

**C**ouscous. Couscous originated in North Africa and is a fine semolina made from wheat. However, variations on the traditional dish can be found in Sicily, France and even Brazil, where it is cuscuz rather than couscous. It is readily available in packages much the same as rice and is served as an accompaniment to a meal. The name couscous applies both to the uncooked granules and the finished dish.

**F**ructose. Often called fruit sugar, it is the sugar found in fruit juices, honey and flower nectar. It can be used in place of ordinary sugar and is sometimes recommended by health experts as it is believed to have nutritional benefits.

**M**alt extract. To make malt extract, the soluble part of the malted grain is extracted and boiled. It is used in homemade beers and wines, hot or cold milky drinks and sometimes in baking.

**M**iso. A fermented soy bean paste used in the Japanese miso soup. You should be aware that most varieties have added salt.

**N**atural foods. Foods sold as containing no added preservatives, emulsifiers or artificial ingredients.

**O**rganic foods. Foods grown without pesticides or synthetic chemical fertilizers.

**S**oy drink. Often called soymilk, it is made from cooked then puréed soybeans. An alternative to cows' milk, it has less calcium than cows' milk. Many commercial varieties are fortified with both calcium and vitamin B12.

**S**oya grits. Precooked soybeans that have been broken up. Taking only a few minutes to cook, they can be added to stews and baked dishes to improve the nutritive value.

**T**ahini. A sesame seed paste, similar to smooth peanut butter. As emulsifiers are not usually added to tahini, it tends to separate and it is necessary to mix in the oil layer before using.

**T**amari. Sometimes called tamari shoyu or Japanese soy sauce. Made only from natural products, soybeans and salt, it contains no MSG (monosodium glutamate), which is often found in Chinese soy sauce.

**T**empeh. A mold-fermented soybean product which looks like tofu. It has a very strong flavor and retains its shape well in cooking. Because of its strong flavor it is not suitable for sweet dishes.

**T**extured Vegetable Protein. TVP is a meat substitute made from soybean concentrate. A concentrated source of protein, it is available in a variety of forms: chips, chunks, granules, crumbs, bits, minced, diced and strips. Some varieties are colored and flavored. It is useful for stews to boost protein content, or in special recipes where it is used as an ingredient.

**T**ofu. A curd or cheese made from soybeans. Popular in Chinese and Japanese cuisine, it has a bland flavor and is easily digested. High in protein, tofu is often used for baked dishes, stuffings and desserts.

**W**hole foods. Foods that are grown or raised in the natural way – for example, free-range eggs.

**Y**east extracts. These are very nutritious and are mostly used in sandwiches and hot savory drinks. Yeast extracts can also be used to flavor soups and stews.

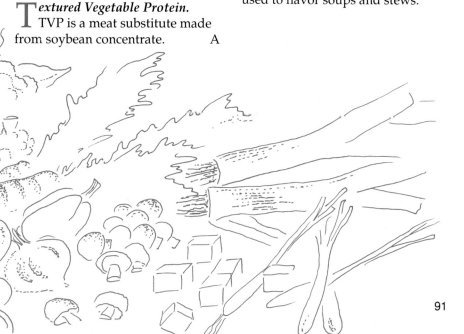

# GLOSSARY

**Arborio rice**     The classic risotto rice from Piedmont. If unavailable use any good quality risotto rice.

**Baby yellow squash**     If unavailable use yellow zucchini or patty pan squash cut into chunks.

**Balsamic vinegar**     A vinegar from Modena aged in wood to become syrupy and luscious. Substitute with red wine vinegar and sugar to taste.

**Bocconcini cheese**     Small balls of fresh mozzarella cheese. If unavailable use fresh mozzarella cut into cubes

**Bread crumbs, dried**     Use commercially packaged bread crumbs.

**Bread crumbs, fresh**     1- or 2-day old bread made into crumbs.

**Catsup**     Tomato sauce.

**Chili sauce**     A sauce which includes chilies, salt and vinegar.

**Cornstarch**     Substitute arrowroot.

**Coconut cream**     Available canned from specialty food shops. Chopped cream coconut, dissolved in boiling water to make a thick cream, may be substituted.

**Coconut milk**     Available canned or as a powder which is reconstituted. Coconut milk may also be made by dissolving 2 oz (60 g) creamed coconut in 5 fl oz (155 mL) boiling water.

**Evaporated skim milk**     Use light or partially skimmed evaporated milk.

**Filo pastry**     A very thin ready-rolled pastry used extensively in Eastern Europe and the Middle East. Available in several sizes. The large sheets, approximately 11 x 18$^{1}$/2-inch (28 x 47 cm) are used in this book.

**Mignonette lettuce**     Gem lettuce

**Muffin pans**     Deep tartlet tins

**Patty pan**     A sheet of tartlet tins

**Reduced fat cream**     Coffee cream

**Rocket**     Arugula, an old-fashioned salad herb, with a peppery taste, which is enjoying a revival. If unavailable use watercress.

**Sour cream**     Commercially soured cream

**Sweet potato**     Orange-fleshed, known as red sweet potato

**Three bean mix**     Canned unseasoned mixed beans

**Wonton wrappers**     Very thin sheets of dough available from Chinese delicatessens used for egg (spring) rolls

# USEFUL INFORMATION

*In this book, ingredients are given in oz and pounds and the nearest equivalent in grams or mL so you know how much to buy. A small inexpensive set of kitchen scales is always handy and very easy to use. Other ingredients in our recipes are given in spoons and cups, so you will need a set of measuring spoons (1 tablespoon, 1 teaspoon, ¹/2 teaspoon and ¹/4 teaspoon), a set of dry measuring cups (1 cup, ¹/2 cup, ¹/3 cup, ¹/4 cup) and a transparent graduated measuring jug (1 quart or 250 mL) for measuring liquids. Spoon and cup measures are level.*

## MEASURING UP

### Metric Measuring Cups

| | | |
|---|---|---|
| 60 mL | 2 fl oz | ¹/4 cup |
| 80 mL | 2¹/2 fl oz | ¹/3 cup |
| 125 mL | 4 fl oz | ¹/2 cup |
| 250 mL | 8 fl oz | 1 cup |

### Metric Measuring Spoons

| | |
|---|---|
| ¹/4 teaspoon | 1.25 mL |
| ¹/2 teaspoon | 2.5 mL |
| 1 teaspoon | 5 mL |
| 1 tablespoon | 20 mL |

## OVEN TEMPERATURES

| °C | °F | Gas Mark |
|---|---|---|
| 120 | 250 | ¹/2 |
| 140 | 275 | 1 |
| 150 | 300 | 2 |
| 160 | 325 | 3 |
| 180 | 350 | 4 |
| 190 | 375 | 5 |
| 200 | 400 | 6 |
| 220 | 425 | 7 |
| 240 | 475 | 8 |
| 250 | 500 | 9 |

## MEASURING DRY INGREDIENTS

| Metric | Imperial |
|---|---|
| 15 g | ¹/2 oz |
| 30 g | 1 oz |
| 60 g | 2 oz |
| 90 g | 3 oz |
| 125 g | 4 oz |
| 155 g | 5 oz |
| 185 g | 6 oz |
| 220 g | 7 oz |
| 250 g | 8 oz |
| 280 g | 9 oz |
| 315 g | 10 oz |
| 350 g | 11 oz |
| 375 g | 12 oz |
| 410 g | 13 oz |
| 440 g | 14 oz |
| 470 g | 15 oz |
| 500 g | 16 oz (1 lb) |
| 750 g | 1 lb 8 oz |
| 1 kg | 2 lb |
| 1.5 kg | 3 lb |
| 2 kg | 4 lb |
| 2.5 kg | 5 lb |

## MEASURING LIQUIDS

| Metric | Imperial | Cup |
|---|---|---|
| 30 mL | 1 fl oz | |
| 60 mL | 2 fl oz | ¹/4 cup |
| 90 mL | 3 fl oz | |
| 125 mL | 4 fl oz | ¹/2 cup |
| 155 mL | 5 fl oz | |
| 170 mL | 5¹/2 fl oz | ²/3 cup |
| 185 mL | 6 fl oz | |
| 220 mL | 7 fl oz | |
| 250 mL | 8 fl oz | 1 cup |
| 500 mL | 16 fl oz | 2 cups |
| 600 mL | 20 fl oz (1 pt) | |
| 750 mL | 1¹/4 pt | |
| 1 litre | 1³/4 pt | 4 cups |
| 1.2 litres | 2 pt | |
| 1.5 litres | 2¹/2 pt | |
| 1.8 litres | 3 pt | |
| 2 litres | 3¹/2 pt | |
| 2.5 litres | 4 pt | |

## QUICK CONVERTER

| Metric | Imperial |
|---|---|
| 5 mm | ¹/4 in |
| 1 cm | ¹/2 in |
| 2 cm | ³/4 in |
| 2.5 cm | 1 in |
| 5 cm | 2 in |
| 10 cm | 4 in |
| 15 cm | 6 in |
| 20 cm | 8 in |
| 23 cm | 9 in |
| 25 cm | 10 in |
| 30 cm | 12 in |

# INDEX

## ACKNOWLEDGMENTS

The publishers wish to thank the following: Admiral Appliances; Black & Decker (Australasia) Pty Ltd; Blanco Appliances; Knebel Kitchens; Leigh Mardon Pty Ltd; Master Foods of Australia; Meadow Lea Foods; Namco Cookware; Ricegrowers' Co-op Mills Ltd; Sunbeam Corporation Ltd; Tycraft Pty Ltd, distributors of Braun, Australia; White Wings Foods for their assistance during recipe testing.

Penny Cox and Meg Thorley for their help during recipe testing.

Donna Hay for her assistance during photography.